THE

FORMEOFCUR Y.

... fome [1] of cury [2] was compiled of the chef Maister Cokes of kyng Richard the Secunde kyng of .nglond [3] aftir the Conquest. the which was acounted þe [4] best and ryallest vyand [5] of alle csten .ynges [6] and it was compiled by assent and avysement of Maisters and [7] phisik [8] and of philosophie þat dwellid in his court. First it techiþ a man for to make commune potages and commune meetis for howshold as þey shold be made craftly and holsomly. Aftirward it techiþ for to make curious potages & meetes and sotiltees [9] for alle maner of States bothe hye and lowe. And the techyng of the forme of making of potages & of meetes bothe of flessh and of fissh. buth [10] y sette here by noumbre and by ordre. sso þis little table here sewyng [11] wole teche a man with oute taryyng: to fynde what meete þat hym lust for to have.

or [12] to make gronnden benes . . . . . I.
For to make drawen benes. . . . . II.
for to make grewel forced.. . . . . III.
Caboches in potage. . . . . IIII.
rapes in potage . . . . V.
Eowtes of Flessh. . . . . VI.
hebolas . . . . VII.
Gowrdes in potage . . . . VIII.

ryse of Flessh.............IX.
Funges...................X.
Bursen..................XI.
Corat...................XII.
noumbles................XIII.
Roobroth................XIIII.
Tredure.................XV.
Mounchelet..............XVI.
Bukkenade...............XVII.
Connat..................XVIII.
drepee..................XIX.
Mawmenee................XX.
Egurdouce...............XXI.
Capouns in Conney...........XXII.
haares in talbotes..........XXIII.
Haares in papdele..........XXIIII.
connynges in Cynee..........XXV.
Connynges in gravey.........XXVI.
Chykens in gravey...........XXVII.
filetes in galyntyne..........XXVIII.
Pigges in sawse sawge.........XXIX.
sawse madame..............XXX.
Gees in hoggepot...........XXXI.
carnel of pork.............XXXII.
Chikens in Caudell..........XXXIII.
chikens in hocchee..........XXXIII.
For to boyle Fesauntes, Partyches
Capons and Curlewes..........XXX. V.
blank manng..............XXXVI.
Blank Dessorre............XXXVII.

morree.	XXXVIII.
Charlet	XXXIX.
charlot y forced.	XX.II.
Cawdel ferry.	XX.II. I.
iusshell.	XX.II. III.[13]
Iusshell enforced	XX.II. IIII.
mortrews.	XX.II. V.
Blank mortrews.	XX.II. VI.
brewet of almony.	XX.II. VII.
Peions y stewed	XX.II. VIII.
loseyns	XX.II. IX.
Tartletes	XX.II. X.
pynnonade	XX.II. XI.
Rosee	XX.II. XII.
cormarye.	XX.II. XIII.
New noumbles of Deer.	XX.II. XIIII.
nota.	XX.II. XV.
Nota.	XX.II. XVI.
ipynee.	XX.II. XVII.
Chyryse	XX.II. XVIII.
payn Foundewe	XX.II. XIX.
Crotoun	XX.III.
vyne grace.	XX.III. I.
Fonnell	XX.III. II.
douce ame	XX.III. III.
Connynges in Cirypp	XX.III. IIII.
leche lumbard	XX.III. V.
Connynges in clere broth.	XX.III. VI.
payn Ragoun	XX.III. VII.
Lete lardes	XX.III. VIII.

furmente with porpeys . . . . XX.III. IX.
Perrey of Pesoun. . . . . XX.III. X.
pesoun of Almayn. . . . . XX.III. XI.
Chiches . . . . XX.III. XII.
frenche owtes . . . . XX.III. XIII.
Makke . . . . XX.III. XIIII.
Aquapates . . . . XX.III. XV.
Salat . . . . XX.III. XVI.
fenkel in soppes. . . . . XX.III. XVII.
Clat. XX.III. XVIII.
appulmoy. . . . . XX.III. XIX.
Slete soppes. . . . . XX.IIII.
Letelorye . . . . XX.IIII. I.
Sowpes Dorry. . . . . XX.IIII. II.
Rapey . . . . XX.IIII. III.
Sause Sarzyne . . . . XX.IIII. IIII.
creme of almanndes. . . . . XX.IIII. V.
Grewel of almandes. . . . . XX.IIII. VI.
cawdel of almandes mylk . . . . XX.IIII. VII.
Iowtes of almannd mylk. . . . . XX.IIII. VIII.
Fygey . . . . XX.IIII. IX.
Pochee. . . . . XX.IIII. X.
brewet of ayrenn. . . . . XX.IIII. XI.
Macrows . . . . XX.IIII. XII.
Tostee. . . . . XX.IIII. XIII.
Gyndawdry . . . . XX.IIII. XIIII.
Erbowle . . . . XX.IIII. XV.
Resmolle. . . . . XX.IIII. XVI.
vyannde Cipre . . . . XX.IIII. XVII.
Vyannde Cipre of Samon. . . . . XX.IIII. XVIII.

vyannde Ryal. . . . . XX.IIII. IX.
Compost . . . . C.
gelee of Fyssh. . . . . C. I.
Gelee of flessh . . . . C. II.
Chysanne. . . . . C. III.
congur in sawce . . . . C. IIII.
Rygh in sawce . . . . C. V.
makerel in sawce. . . . . C. VI.
Pykes in brasey . . . . C. VII.
porpeys in broth. . . . . C. VIII.
Ballok broth. . . . . C. IX.
eles in brewet. . . . . C. X
Cawdel of Samoun. . . . . C. XI.
plays in Cynee. . . . . C. XII.
For to make Flaumpeyns. . . . . C. XIII.
for to make noumbles in lent. . . . . . . C. XIIII.
For to make Chawdoun for lent . . . . . . C. XV.
furmente with porpays . . . . C. XVI.
Fylettes in galyntyne . . . . C. XVII.
veel in buknade . . . . C. XVIII.
Sooles in Cyney . . . . C. IX.
tenches in Cyney. . . . . XX.VI.
Oysters in gravey . . . . XX.VI. I
muskels in brewet . . . . XX.VI. II
Oysters in Cyney. . . . . XX.VI. III.
cawdel of muskels . . . . XX.VI. IIII.
Mortrews of Fyssh . . . . XX.VI. V
laumpreys in galyntyne. . . . . XX.VI. VI.
Laumprouns in galyntyne . . . . XX.VI. VII.
losyns in Fysshe day. . . . . XX.VI. VIII.

Sowpes in galyntyne . . . . XX.VI. IX.
sobre sawse . . . . XX.VI. X.
Colde Brewet. . . . . XX.VI. XI.
peeres in confyt. . . . . XX.VI. XII.
Egur douce of Fyssh . . . . XX.VI. XIII.
Cold Brewet . . . . XX.VI. XIIII.
Pevorat for Veel and Venysoun . . . . . . XX.VI. XV.
sawce blaunche for Capouns y sode . . . . XX.VI. XVI.
Sawce Noyre for Capons y rosted . . . . . XX.VI. XVII.
Galentyne . . . . XX.VI. XVIII.
Gyngeuer. . . . . XX.VI. XIX.
verde sawse . . . . XX.VII.
Sawce Noyre for mallard . . . . XX.VII. I.
cawdel for Gees . . . . XX.VII. II.
Chawdon for Swannes . . . . XX.VII. III.
sawce Camelyne. . . . . XX.VII. IIII.
Lumbard Mustard . . . . XX.VII. V.
Nota. . . . . XX.VII. VI.
Nota. . . . . XX.VII. VII.
frytour blaunched . . . . XX.VII. VIII.
Frytour of pasturnakes. . . . . XX.VII. IX.

   frytour of mylke. . . . . XX.VII. X.
frytour of Erbes. . . . . XX.VII. XI.
Raisiowls . . . . XX.VII. XII.
Whyte milates . . . . XX.VII. XIII.
crustardes of flessh. . . . . XX.VII. XIIII.
Mylates of Pork . . . . XX.VII. XV.
crustardes of Fyssh . . . . XX.VII. XVI.
Crustardes of erbis on fyssh day. . . . . XX.VII. XVII.

lesshes fryed in lentoun.	XX.VII. XVIII.
Wastels y farced.	XX.VII. XIX.
sawge y farced.	XX.VIII.
Sawgeat	XX.VIII. I.
cryspes	XX.VIII. II.
Cryspels.	XX.VIII. III.
Tartee.	XX.VIII. IIII.
Tart in Ymbre day	XX.VIII. V.
tart de Bry	XX.VIII. VI.
Tart de Brymlent.	XX.VIII. VII.
tartes of Flessh.	XX.VIII. VIII.
Tartletes	XX.VIII. IX.
tartes of Fyssh	XX.VIII. X.
Sambocade	XX.VIII. XI.
Erbolat	XX.VIII. XII.
Nysebek	XX.VIII. XIII.
for to make Pom Dorryes. & oþer þynges.	XX.VIII. XIIII.
Cotagres.	XX.VIII. XV.
hart rows	XX.VIII. XVI.
Potews.	XX.VIII. XVII.
Sachus.	XX.VIII. XVIII.
Bursews	XX.VIII. XIX.
spynoches y fryed	XX.IX.
Benes y fryed	XX.IX. I.
russhewses of Fruyt	XX.IX. II.
Daryols	XX.IX. III.
Flaumpens	XX.IX. IIII.
Chewetes on flessh day.	XX.IX. V.

comadore. . . . . XX.IX. VIII.
Chastletes. . . . . XX.IX. IX.
for to make twey pecys of Flesshe
to fasten to gydre. . . . . XX.IX. X.
pur fait y pocras . . . . XX.IX. XI.
For to make blank maunnger. . . . . XX.IX. XII.
for to make Blank Desire. . . . . XX.IX. XIII.
For to make mawmoune. . . . . XX.IX. XIIII.
the pety peruaunt . . . . XX.IX. XV.
And the pete puant. . . . . XX.IX. XVI.

FOR TO MAKE GRONDEN BENES [1]. I.

Take benes and dry hem in a nost [2] or in an Ovene and hulle hem wele and wyndewe [3] out þe hulk and wayshe hem clene an do hem to seeþ in gode broth [4] an ete hem with Bacon.

[1] Gronden Benes. Beans ground (y ground, as No. 27. 53. 105.) stript of their hulls. This was a dish of the poorer householder, as also is 4 and 5, and some others. [2] a nost. An ost, or kiln. Vide Gloss. *voce* Ost. [3] wyndewe. Winnow. [4] gode broth. Prepared beforehand.

FOR TO MAKE DRAWEN BENES. II.

Take benes and seeþ hem and grynde hem in a morter [1] and drawe hem up [2] with gode broth an do Oynouns in the broth grete mynced [3] an do þerto and colour it with Safroun and serve it forth.

[1] morter. Mortar. [2] drawen hem up. Mix them. [3] grete mynced. Grossly, not too small.

FOR TO MAKE GREWEL FORCED [1]. III.

Take grewel and do to the fyre with gode flessh and seeþ it wel. take the lire [2] of Pork and grynd it smal [3] and drawe the grewel thurgh a Straynour

[4] and colour it wiþ Safroun and serue [5] forth.

[1] forced, farced, enriched with flesh. Vide Gloss. [2] lire. Flesh. [3] grynd it smal. Bruise or beat in a mortar. [4] stryno'. Strainer. [5] serue. Serve. Vide Gloss.

CABOCHES [1] IN POTAGE. IIII.

Take Caboches and quarter hem and seeth hem in gode broth with Oynouns y mynced and the whyte of Lekes y slyt and corue smale [2] and do þer to safroun an salt and force it with powdour douce [3].

[1] Caboches. Probably cabbages. [2] corue smale. Cut small. V. *i corue* in Gloss. [3] powdour douce. Sweet aromatic powder. V. Pref.

RAPES [1] IN POTAGE. V.

Take rapus and make hem clene and waissh hem clene. quare hem [2]. parboile hem. take hem up. cast hem in a gode broth and seeþ hem. mynce Oynouns and cast þerto Safroun and salt and messe it forth with powdour douce. the wise [3] make of Pasturnakes [4] and skyrwates. [5]

[1] Rapes, or rapus. Turneps. [2] quare hem. Cut them in *squares*, or small pieces. V. Gloss. [3] in the wise, *i.e.* in the same manner. *Self* or *same*, seems to be casually omitted. Vide No. 11 and 122. [4] Pasturnakes, for parsnips or carrots. V. Gloss. [5] skyrwates, for skirrits or skirwicks.

EOWTES [1] OF FLESSH. VI.

Take Borage. cool [2]. langdebef [3]. persel [4]. betes. orage [5]. auance [6]. violet [7]. saueray [8]. and fenkel [9]. and whane þey buth sode; presse hem wel smale. cast hem in gode broth an seeþ hem. and serue hem forth.

[1] Eowtes. *Lowtes*, No. 88, where, in the process, it is *Rowtes*. Quære the meaning, as Roots does not apply to the matter of the Recipe. In No. 73 it is written *owtes*. [2] Cole, or colewort. [3] Langdebef. Bugloss, buglossum sylvestre. These names all arise from a similitude to an ox's tongue. V. Ms. Ed. No. 43. [4] Persel. Parsley. [5] orage. Orach, *Atriplex*. Miller, Gard. Dict. [6] auance. Fortè Avens. V. Avens, in Gloss. [7] The leaves probably, and not the flower. [8] Savory. [9] Fenkel. Fennil.

HEBOLACE [1]. VII.

Take Oynouns and erbes and hewe hem small and do þes to gode broth. and aray [2] it as þou didest caboches. If þey be in fyssh day. make [3] on the same maner [4] with water and oyle. and if it be not in Lent alye [5] it with zolkes of Eyren [6]. and dresse it forth and cast þer to powdour douce.

[1] Hebolace. Contents, Hebolas; for *Herbolas*, from the herbs used; or, if the first letter be omitted (see the Contents), *Chebolas*, from the Chibols employed. [2] aray. Dress, set it out. [3] make. Dress. Vide Gloss. [4] maner. manner. [5] alye. Mix. V. Gloss. [6] Eyren. Eggs. V. Gloss.

GOURDES IN POTAGE. VIII.

Take young Gowrdes pare hem and kerue [1] hem on pecys. cast hem in gode broth, and do þer to a gode pertye [2] of Oynouns mynced. take Pork soden. grynd it and alye it þer with and wiþ zolkes of ayrenn. do þer to safroun and salt, and messe it forth with powdour douce.

[1] kerve. Cut. [2] partye. Party, i.e. quantity.

RYSE [1] OF FLESH. IX.

Take Ryse and waishe hem clene. and do hem in erthen pot with gode

broth and lat hem seeþ wel. afterward take Almaund mylke [2] and do þer to. and colour it wiþ safroun an salt, an messe forth.

[1] Ryse. Rice. V. Gloss. [2] Almand mylke. V. Gloss.

FUNGES [1]. X.

Take Funges and pare hem clere and dyce hem [2]. take leke and shred hym small and do hym to seeþ in gode broth. colour it with safron and do þer inne powdour fort [3].

[1] Funges. Mushrooms. [2] dyce hem. Cut them in squares. Vide *quare* in Gloss. [3] Powdour fort. Vide Preface.

BURSEN [1]. XI.

Take the whyte of Lekes. slype hem and shrede hem small. take Noumbles [2] of swyne and boyle hem in broth and wyne. take hym up and dresse hem and do the Leke in the broth. seeþ and do the Noumbles þer to make a Lyour [3] of brode blode and vynegre and do þer to Powdour fort seeþ Oynouns mynce hem and do þer to. the self wise make of Pigges.

[1] Bursen. Qu. the etymon. [2] Noumbles. Entrails. V. Gloss. [3] Lyo', Lyour. A mixture. Vide *alye* in Gloss.

CORAT [1]. XII.

Take the Noumbles of Calf. Swyne. or of Shepe. parboile hem and skerne hem to dyce [2] cast hem in gode broth and do þer to erbes. grynde chyballes [3]. smale y hewe. seeþ it tendre and lye it with zolkes of eyrenn. do þer to verious [4] safroun powdour douce and salt, and serue it forth.

   [1] Corat. Qu. [2] kerve hem to dyce. V. *quare* in Gloss. [3] Chyballes. Chibols, young onions. V. Gloss. [4] verious. Verjuice.

NOUMBLES. XIII.

Take noumbles of Deer oþer [1] of oþer beest parboile hem kerf hem to dyce. take the self broth or better. take brede and grynde with the broth. and temper it [2] up with a gode quantite of vyneger and wyne. take the oynouns and parboyle hem. and mynce hem smale and do þer to. colour it with blode and do þer to powdour fort and salt and boyle it wele and serue it fort [3].

   [1] oþer. Other, i.e. or. [2] temper it. Temper it, i. e. mix it. [3] fort. Miswritten for *forth*. So again No. 31. 127.

ROO [1] BROTH. XIIII.

Take the lire of the Deer oþer of the Roo parboile it on smale peces. seeþ it wel half in water and half in wyne. take brede and bray it wiþ the self broth and drawe blode þer to and lat it seeth to gedre with powdour fort of gynger oþer of canell [2]. and macys [3]. with a grete porcioun of vineger with Raysouns of Coraunte [4].

[1] Roo. Roe. The Recipe in Ms. Ed. No. 53. is very different. [2] Canell. Cinnamon. [3] macys. Mace. V. Preface and Gloss. [4] Raysouns of Coraunte. Currants. V. Gloss.

TREDURE [1]. XV.

Take Brede and grate it. make a lyre [2] of rawe ayrenn and do þerto Safroun and powdour douce. and lye it up [3] with gode broth. and make it as a Cawdel. and do þerto a lytel verious.

[1] Tredure. A Cawdle; but quære the etymon. The French *tresdur e* does not seem to answer. [2] lyre. Mixture. [3] lye it up. Mix it.

MONCHELET [1]. XVI.

Take Veel oþer Moton and smite it to gobettes seeþ it in gode broth. cast þerto erbes yhewe [2] gode wyne. and a quantite of Oynouns mynced. Powdour fort and Safroun. and alye it with ayren and verious. but lat not seeþ after.

[1] Monchelet. *Mounchelet*, Contents. [2] y hewe. Shred.

BUKKENADE [1]. XVII.

Take Hennes [2] oþer Conynges [3] oþer Veel oþer oþer Flessh an hewe hem to gobettes waische it and hit well [4]. grynde Almandes unblaunched. and drawe hem up with þe broth cast þer inne raysons of Corance. sugur. Powdour gyngur erbes ystewed in grees [5]. Oynouns and Salt. If it is to to [6] thynne. alye it up with flour of ryse oþer with oþer thyng and colour it with Safroun.

[1] Bukkenade. Vide No. 118. qu. [2] Hennes; including, I suppose, chicken and pullets. [3] Conynges. Coneys, Rabbits. [4] hit well. This makes no sense, unless *hit* signifies smite or beat. [5] Grees. Fat, lard, *grece*. No. 19. [6] to to. So again, No. 124. To is *too*, v. Gloss. And *too* is found doubled in this manner in *Mirrour for Magistrates*, p. 277. 371, and other authors.

CONNATES [1]. XVIII.

Take Connes and pare hem. pyke out the best and do hem in a pot of erthe. do þerto whyte grece þat he stewe þer inne. and lye hem up with hony clarified and with rawe zolkes [2] and with a lytell almaund mylke and do þerinne powdour fort and Safron. and loke þat it be yleesshed [3],

[1] Connat seems to be a kind of marmalade of connes, or quinces, from Fr. *Coing*. Chaucer, v. Coines. Written quinces No. 30. [2] Yolkes, i. e. of Eggs. [3] yleesshed. V. Gloss.

DREPEE [1]. XIX.

Take blanched Almandes grynde hem and temper hem up with gode broth take Oynouns a grete quantite parboyle hem and frye hem and do þerto. take smale bryddes [2] parboyle hem and do þerto Pellydore [3] and salt. and a lytel grece.

[1] Drepee. Qu. [2] bryddes. Birds. *Per metathesin; v. R. in Indice.* [3] Pellydore. Perhaps *pellitory. Peletour*, 104.

Mawmenee [1]. XX.

Take a pottel of wyne greke. and ii. pounde of sugur take and clarifye the sugur with a qantite of wyne an drawe it thurgh a straynour in to a pot of erthe take flour of Canell [2]. and medle [3] with sum of the wyne an cast to gydre. take pynes [4] with Dates and frye hem a litell in grece oþer in oyle and cast hem to gydre. take clowes [5] an flour of canel hool [6] and cast þerto. take powdour gyngur. canel. clower, colour it with saundres a lytel yf hit be nede cast salt þerto. and lat it seeþ; warly [7] with a slowe fyre and not to thyk [8], take brawn [9] of Capouns yteysed [10]. oþer of Fesauntes teysed small and cast þerto.

[1] Vide No. 194, where it is called *Mawmenny.* [2] Flour of Canell. Powder of Cinamon. [3] medle. Mix. [4] pynes. A nut, or fruit. Vide Gloss. [5] clowes. Cloves. [6] hool. Whole. How can it be the flour, or powder, if whole? Quære, *flower* of cand for *mace.* [7] warly. Warily, gently. [8] not to thyk. So as to be too thick; or perhaps, *not to thicken.* [9] brawn. Fleshy part. Few Capons are cut now except about Darking in Surry; they have been excluded by the turkey, a more magnificent, but perhaps not a better fowl.

[10] yteysed, or *teysed,* as afterwards. Pulled in pieces by the fingers, called *teezing* No. 36. This is done now with flesh of turkeys, and thought better than mincing. Vide Junius, voce *Tease.*

EGURDOUCE [1]. XXI.

Take Conynges or Kydde and smyte hem on pecys rawe. and frye hem in white grece. take raysouns of Coraunce and fry hem take oynouns parboile hem and hewe hem small and fry hem. take rede wyne suger with powdour of peper. of gynger of canel. salt. and cast þerto. and lat it seeþ with a gode quantite of white grece an serue it forth.

[1] Egurdouce. The term expresses *piccantedolce*, a mixture of sour and sweet; but there is nothing of the former in the composition. Vide Gloss.

CAPOUNS IN COUNCYS [1]. XXII.

Take Capons and rost hem right hoot þat þey be not half y nouhz and hewe hem to gobettes and cast hem in a pot, do þerto clene broth, seeþ hem þat þey be tendre. take brede and þe self broth and drawe it up yferer [2], take strong Powdour and Safroun and Salt and cast þer to. take ayrenn and seeþ hem harde. take out the zolkes and hewe the whyte þerinne, take the Pot fro þe fyre and cast the whyte þerinne. messe the disshes þerwith and lay the zolkes hool and flour it with clowes.

[1] Concys seems to be a kind of known sauce. V. Gloss. [2] yfere. Together.

HARES [1] IN TALBOTES [2]. XXIII.

Take Hares and hewe hem to gobettes and seeþ hem with þe blode unwaisshed in broth. and whan þey buth y nowh: cast hem in colde water. pyke and waisshe hem clene. cole [3] the broth and drawe it thurgh a straynour. take oþer blode and cast in boylyng water seeþ it and drawe it thurgh a straynour. take Almaundes unblaunched. waisshe hem and grynde hem and temper it up with the self broth. cast al in a pot. tak oynouns and parboile hem smyte hem small and cast hem in to þis Pot. cast þerinne Powdour fort. vynegur an salt.

[1] Haares, Contents. So again, No. 24. [2] Talbotes. Ms. Ed. No. 9, *Talbotays*. [3] Cole. Cool.

HARES IN PAPDELE [1]. XXIIII.

Take Hares parboile hem in gode broth. cole the broth and waisshe the fleyssh. cast azeyn [2] to gydre. take obleys [3] oþer wafrouns [4] in stede of lozeyns [5]. and cowche [6] in dysshes. take powdour douce and lay on salt the broth and lay onoward [7] an messe forth.

[1] Papdele. Qu. [2] azeyn. Again. [3] obleys, called *oblatæ*; for which see Hearne ad Lib. Nig. I. p. 344. A kind of Wafer, otherwise called *Nebulæ*; and is the French *oublie,oble* . Leland, Collect. IV. p. 190. 327. [4] wafrouns. Wafers. [5] loseyns. Vide Gloss. [6] cowche. Lay. [7] onoward. Upon it.

CONNYNGES IN CYNEE [1]. XXV.

Take Connynges and smyte hem on peces. and seeþ hem in gode broth, mynce Oynouns and seeþ hem in grece and in gode broth do þerto. drawe a lyre of brede. blode. vynegur and broth do þerto with powdour fort.

[1] Cynee. Vide Gloss.

CONNYNGES IN GRAUEY. XXVI.

Take Connynges smyte hem to pecys. parboile hem and drawe hem with a gode broth with almandes blanched and brayed. do þerinne sugur and powdour gynger and boyle it and the flessh þerwith. flour it with sugur and with powdour gynger an serue forth.

CHYKENS IN GRAVEY. XXVII.

Take Chykens and serue hem the same manere and serue forth.

FYLETTES [1] OF GALYNTYNE [2]. XXVIII.

Take fylettes of Pork and rost hem half ynowh smyte hem on pecys. drawe a lyour of brede and blode. and broth and Vineger. and do þerinne. seeþ it wele. and do þerinne powdour an salt an messe it forth.

[1] Fylettes. Fillets. [2] of Galyntyne. In Galyntyne. Contents, *rectlus*. As for *Galentine*, see the Gloss.

PYGGES IN SAWSE SAWGE [1]. XXIX.

Take Pigges yskaldid and quarter hem and seeþ hem in water and salt, take hem and lat hem kele [2]. take persel sawge. and grynde it with brede and zolkes of ayrenn harde ysode. temper it up with vyneger sum what thyk. and, lay the Pygges in a vessell. and the sewe onoward and serue it forth.

[1] Sawge. Sage. As several of them are to be used, these pigs must have been small. [2] kele. Cool.

SAWSE MADAME. XXX.

Take sawge. persel. ysope. and saueray. quinces. and peeres [1], garlek and Grapes. and fylle the gees þerwith. and sowe the hole þat no grece come out. and roost hem wel. and kepe the grece þat fallith þerof. take galytyne and grece and do in a possynet, whan the gees buth rosted ynowh; take an smyte hem on pecys. and þat tat [2] is withinne and do it in a possynet and put þerinne wyne if it be to thyk. do þerto powdour of galyngale. powdour douce and salt and boyle the sawse and dresse þe Gees in disshes and lay þe sowe onoward.

[1] Peares. Pears. [2] that tat, i.e. that that. Vide Gloss.

GEES IN HOGGEPOT [1]. XXXI.

Take Gees and smyte hem on pecys. cast hem in a Pot do þerto half wyne and half water. and do þerto a gode quantite of Oynouns and erbest. Set it ouere the fyre and couere [2] it fast. make a layour of brede and blode an lay it þerwith. do þerto powdour fort and serue it fort.

[1] Hoggepot. Hodge-podge. *Ochepot.* Ms. Ed. No. 22. French, *Hochepot.* Cotgrave. See Junii Enym. v. *Hotch-potch.* [2] couere. Cover.

CARNEL [1] OF PORK. XXXII.

Take the brawnn of Swyne. parboile it and grynde it smale and alay it up with zolkes of ayren. set it ouere [2] the fyre with white Grece and lat it not seeþ to fast. do þerinne Safroun an powdour fort and messe it forth. and cast þerinne powdour douce, and serue it forth.

[1] Carnel, perhaps *Charnel,* from Fr. *Chaire.* [2] ouere. Over. So again, No. 33.

CHYKENNS [1] IN CAWDEL. XXXIII.

Take Chikenns and boile hem in gode broth and ramme [2] hem up. þenne take zolkes of ayrenn an þe broth and alye it togedre. do þerto powdour of gynger and sugur ynowh safroun and salt. and set it ouere the fyre withoute boyllyng. and serue the Chykenns hole [3] oþer ybroke and lay þe sowe onoward.

[1] Chikens. Contents. So again in the next Recipe. [2] ramme. Qu. press them close together. [3] hole. Whole.

CHYKENS IN HOCCHEE [1]. XXXIIII.

Take Chykenns and scald hem. take parsel and sawge withoute eny oþere erbes. take garlec an grapes and stoppe the Chikenns ful and seeþ hem in gode broth. so þat þey may esely be boyled þerinne. messe hem an cast þerto powdour dowce.

[1] Hochee. This does not at all answer to the French *Hachis,* or our *Hash*; therefore qu.

FOR TO BOILE FESAUNTES. PARTRUCHES. CAPONS AND CURLEWES. XXXV.

Take gode broth and do þerto the Fowle. and do þerto hool peper and flour of canel a gode quantite and lat hem seeþ þwith. and messe it forth. and þer cast þeron Podour dowce.

BLANK MAUNGER [1]. XXXVI.

Take Capouns and seeþ hem, þenne take hem up. take Almandes blaunched. grynd hem and alay hem up with the same broth. cast the mylk in a pot. waisshe rys and do þerto and lat it seeþ. þanne take brawn of Capouns teere it small and do þerto. take white grece sugur and salt and cast þerinne. lat it seeþ. þenne messe it forth and florissh it with aneys in confyt rede oþer whyt. and with Almaundes fryed in oyle. and serue it forth.

[1] Blank Maunger. Very different from ours. Vide Gloss.

BLANK DESSORRE [1]. XXXVII.

Take Almandes blaunched, grynde hem and temper hem up with whyte wyne, on fleissh day with broth. and cast þerinne flour of Rys. oþer amydoun [2], and lye it þerwith. take brawn of Capouns yground. take sugur and salt and cast þerto and florissh it with aneys whyte. take a vessel yholes [3] and put in safroun. and serue it forth.

[1] Blank Dessorre. V. Gloss. [2] Amydoun. "Fine wheat flour steeped in water, strained and let stand to settle, then drained and dried in the sun; used for bread or in broths." Cotgrave. Used in No. 68 for colouring white. [3] yholes. Quære.

MORREE [1]. XXXVIII.

Take Almandes blaunched, waisshe hem. grynde hem. and temper hem up with rede wyne, and alye hem with flour of Rys. do þerto Pynes yfryed. and colour it with saundres. do þerto powdour fort and powdour douce

and salt, messe it forth and flour it [2] with aneys confyt whyte.

[1] Morree. Ms. Ed. 37. *murrey*. Ibid. II. 26. *morrey*; probably from the mulberries used therein. [2] flour it. Flourish it.

CHARLET [1]. XXXIX.

Take Pork and seeþ it wel. hewe it smale. cast it in a panne. breke ayrenn and do þerto and swyng [2] it wel togyder. do þerto Cowe mylke and Safroun and boile it togyder. salt it & messe it forth.

[1] Charlet; probably from the French, *chair*. Qu. Minced Meat, and the next article, Forced Meat. [2] swyng. Shake, mix.

CHARLET YFORCED. XX.II.

Take mylke and seeþ it, and swyng þerwith zolkes of Ayrenn and do þerto. and powdour of gynger suger. and Safroun and cast þerto. take the Charlet out of the broth and messe it in dysshes, lay the sewe onoward. flour it with powdour douce. and serue it forth.

CAWDEL FERRY [1]. XX.II. I.

Take flour of Payndemayn [2] and gode wyne. and drawe it togydre. do þerto a grete quantite of Sugur cypre. or hony clarified, and do þerto safroun. boile it. and whan it is boiled, alye it up with zolkes of ayrenn. and do þerto salt and messe it forth. and lay þeron sugur and powdour gyngur.

[1] ferry. Quære. We have *Carpe in Ferry*, Lel. Coll. VI. p. 21. [2] Payndemayn. White bread. Chaucer.

JUSSHELL [1]. XX.II. III.

Take brede ygrated and ayrenn and swyng it togydre. do þerto safroun, sawge. and salt. & cast broth. þerto. boile it & messe it forth.

[1] Jusshell. See also next number. *Jussell*, Ms. Ed. 21, where the Recipe is much the same. Lat. *Juscellam*, which occurs in the old scholiast on Juvenal iv. 23; and in Apicius, v. 3. Vide Du Fresne, v. *Jusselium* and *Juscellum*, where the composition consists of *vinum*, *ova*, and *sagmea*, very different from this. Faber in Thesauro cites *Juscellum Gallinæ* from Theod. Priscianus.

N.B. No. XX.II. II. is omitted both here and in the Contents.

JUSSHELL ENFORCED [1]. XX.II. IIII.

Take and do þerto as to charlet yforced. and serue it forth.

[1] Jusshell enforced. As the *Charlet yforced* here referred to was made of pork, compare No. 40 with No. 39. So in Theod. Priscian we have *JussetlumGallinæ* .

MORTREWS [1]. XX.II. V.

Take hennes and Pork and seeþ hem togyder. take the lyre of Hennes and of the Pork, and hewe it small and grinde it all to doust [2]. take brede ygrated and do þerto, and temper it with the self broth and alye it with zolkes of ayrenn, and cast þeron powdour fort, boile it and do þerin powdour of gyngur sugur. safroun and salt. and loke þer it be stondyng [3], and flour it with powdour gynger.

[1] Mortrews. Vide Gloss. [2] doust. Dust, powder. [3] stondyng. Stiff, thick.

MORTREWS BLANK. XX.II. VI.

Take Pork and Hennes and seeþ hem as to fore. bray almandes blaunched, and temper hem up with the self broth. and alye the fleissh with the mylke and white flour of Rys. and boile it. & do þerin powdour of gyngur sugar and look þat it be stondyng.

BREWET OF ALMONY [1]. XX.II. VII.

Take Conynges or kiddes and hewe hem small on moscels [2] oþer on pecys. parboile hem with the same broth, drawe an almaunde mylke and do the fleissh þerwith, cast þerto powdour galyngale & of gynger with flour of Rys. and colour it wiþ alkenet. boile it, salt it. & messe it forth with sugur and powdour douce.

[1] Almony. Almaine, or Germany. *Almany.* Fox, part I. p. 239. *Alamanie.* Chron. Sax. p. 242. V. ad No. 71. [2] moscels. Morsels.

PEIOUNS [1] YSTEWED. XX.II. VIII.

Take peions and stop hem with garlec ypylled and with gode erbes ihewe. and do hem in an erthen pot. cast þerto gode broth and whyte grece. Powdour fort. safroun verious & salt.

[1] Peiouns, Pejons, i. e. Pigeons, *j* is never written here in the middle of a word.

LOSEYNS [1]. XX.II. IX.

Take gode broth and do in an erthen pot, take flour of payndemayn and make þerof past with water. and make þerof thynne foyles as paper [2] with a roller, drye it harde and seeþ it in broth take Chese ruayn [3] grated and lay it in disshes with powdour douce. and lay þeron loseyns isode as hoole as þou mizt [4]. and above powdour and chese, and so twyse or thryse, & serue it forth.

[1] Loseyns. Vide in Gloss. [2] foyles as paper. *Leaves* of paste as thin as *paper*. [3] Chese ruyan. 166. Vide Gloss. [4] mizt. Might, i.e. can.

TARTLETTES [1]. XX.II. X.

Take pork ysode and grynde it small with safroun, medle it with ayrenn and raisons of coraunce and powdour fort and salt, and make a foile of dowhz [2] and close the fars [3] þerinne. cast þe Tartletes in a Panne with faire water boillyng and salt, take of the clene Flessh withoute ayren & bolle it in gode broth. cast þerto powdour douce and salt, and messe the tartletes in disshes & helde [4] the sewe þeronne.

[1] Tarlettes. *Tartletes* in the process. [2] foile of dowhz, or dowght. A leaf of paste. [3] fars. Forced-meat. [4] helde. Cast.

PYNNONADE [1]. XX.II. XI.

Take Almandes iblaunched and drawe hem sumdell thicke [2] with gode broth oþer with water and set on the fire and seeþ it, cast þerto zolkes of ayrenn ydrawe. take Pynes yfryed in oyle oþer in grece and þerto white Powdour douce, sugur and salt. & colour it wiþ alkenet a lytel.

[1] Pynnonade. So named from the *Pynes* therein used. [2] sumdell thicke. Somewhat thick, thickish.

ROSEE [1]. XX.II. XII.

Take thyk mylke as to fore welled [2]. cast þerto sugur a gode porcioun pynes. Dates ymynced. canel. & powdour gynger and seeþ it, and alye it with flores of white Rosis, and flour of rys, cole it, salt it & messe it forth. If þou wilt in stede of Almaunde mylke, take swete cremes of kyne.

[1] Rosee. From the white roles therein mentioned. See No. 41. in Mi. Ed. but No. 47 there is totally different. [2] welled, f. *willed*; directed.

CORMARYE [1]. XX.II. XIII.

Take Colyandre [2], Caraway smale grounden, Powdour of Peper and garlec ygrounde in rede wyne, medle alle þise [3] togyder and salt it, take loynes of Pork rawe and fle of the skyn, and pryk it wel with a knyf and lay it in the sawse, roost þerof what þou wilt, & kepe þat þat fallith þerfro in the rosting and seeþ it in a possynet with faire broth, & serue it forth witþ þe roost anoon [4].

[1] Cormarye. Quære. [2] Golyandre. Coriander. [3] þise. These. [4] anoon. Immediately.

NEWE NOUMBLES OF DEER. XX.II. XIIII.

Take noumbles and waisshe hem clene with water and salt and perboile hem in water. take hem up an dyce hem. do with hem as with ooþer noumbles.

NOTA. XX.II. XV.

The Loyne of the Pork, is fro the hippe boon to the hede.

NOTA. XX.II. XVI.

The fyletes buth two, that buth take oute of the Pestels [1].

[1] Pestels. Legs.

SPYNEE [1]. XX.II.XVII.

Take and make gode thik Almaund mylke as tofore. and do þerin of flour of hawthorn [2]. and make it as a rose. & serue it forth.

[1] Spynee. As made of Haws, the berries of Spines, or Hawthorns. [2] Hawthern. Hawthorn.

CHYRYSE [1] XX.II. XVIII.

Take Almandes unblanched, waisshe hem, grynde hem, drawe hem up with gode broth. do þerto thridde part of chiryse. þe stones. take oute and grynde hem smale, make a layour of gode brede an powdour and salt and do þerto. colour it with sandres so that it may be stondyng, and florish it with aneys and with cheweryes, and strawe þeruppon and serue it forth.

[1] Chyryse. *Chiryse* in the process. *Cheriseye.* Ms. Ed. II. 18. *Chiryes* there are cherries. And this dish is evidently made of Cherries, which probably were chiefly imported at this time from Flanders, though they have a Saxon name, [Anglo-Saxon: cyrre].

PAYN FONDEW [1]. XX.II. XIX.

Take brede and frye it in grece oþer in oyle, take it and lay it in rede wyne. grynde it with raisouns take hony and do it in a pot and cast þerinne gleyres [2] of ayrenn wiþ a litel water and bete it wele togider with a sklyse [3]. set it ouer the fires and boile it. and whan the hatte [4] arisith to goon [5] ouer, take it adoun and kele it, and whan it is þer clarified; do it to the oþere with sugur and spices. salt it and loke it be stondyng, florish it with white coliaundre in confyt.

[1] foundewe. Contents. It seems to mean *dissolved*. V. *found* in Gloss. [2] gleyres. Whites. [3] Sklyse. Slice. [4] hatte. Seems to mean *bubling* or

wallop. [5] goon. Go.

CROTOUN [1]. XX.III.

Take the offal of Capouns oþer of oþere briddes. make hem clene and parboile hem. take hem up and dyce hem. take swete cowe mylke and cast þerinne. and lat it boile. take Payndemayn [2] and of þe self mylke and drawe thurgh a cloth and cast it in a pot and lat it seeþ, take ayren ysode. hewe the white and cast þerto, and alye the sewe with zolkes of ayren rawe. colour it with safron. take the zolkes and fry hem and florish hem þerwith and with powdour douce.

[1] Crotoun. Ms. Ed. 24. has *Craytoun*, but a different dish. [2] Payndemayn. Whitebread. V. ad No. 41.

VYNE GRACE [1]. XX.III. I.

Take smale fylettes of Pork and rost hem half and smyte hem to gobettes and do hem in wyne an Vynegur and Oynouns ymynced and stewe it yfere do þerto gode poudours an salt, an serue it forth.

[1] Vyne Grace. Named probably from *grees*, wild swine, and the mode of dressing in *wine*. V. Gloss. voce *Vynegrace*.

FONNELL [1]. XX.III. II.

Take Almandes unblaunched. grynde hem and drawe hem up with gode broth, take a lombe [2] or a kidde and half rost hym. or the þridde [3] part, smyte hym in gobetes and cast hym to the mylke. take smale briddes yfasted and ystyned [4]. and do þerto sugur, powdour of canell and salt, take zolkes of ayrenn harde ysode and cleeue [5] a two and ypaunced [6] with flour of canell and florish þe sewe above. take alkenet fryed and yfoundred [7] and droppe above with a feþur [8] and messe it forth.

[1] Fonnell. Nothing in the recipe leads to the etymon of this multifarious dish. [2] Lombe. Lamb. [3] thridde. Third, per metathesin. [4] yfasted and ystyned. [5] cleeue. cloven. [6] ypaunced. pounced. [7] yfoundred. melted, dissolved. [8] feþ'. feather.

DOUCE AME [1]. XX.III. III.

Take gode Cowe mylke and do it in a pot. take parsel. sawge. ysope. saueray and ooþer gode herbes. hewe hem and do hem in the mylke and seeþ hem. take capouns half yrosted and smyte hem on pecys and do þerto pynes and hony clarified. salt it and colour it with safroun an serue it forth.

[1] Douce Ame. *Quasi*, a delicious dish. V. Blank Desire in Gloss. Titles of this tissue occur in Apicius. See Humelberg. p. 2.

CONNYNGES IN CYRIP [1]. XX.III. IIII.

Take Connynges and seeþ hem wel in good broth. take wyne greke and do þerto with a porcioun of vyneger and flour of canel, hoole clowes quybibes hoole, and ooþer gode spices with raisouns coraunce and gyngyner ypared and ymynced. take up the conynges and smyte hem on pecys and cast hem into the Siryppe and seeþ hem a litel on the fyre and sue it forth.

[1] Cyrip. In the process *Siryppe. Cirypp*, Contents. *Sirop* or *Sirup*, as 133. *Syryp*, 132.

LECHE LUMBARD [1]. XX.III. V.

Take rawe Pork and pulle of the skyn. and pyke out þe skyn synewes and bray the Pork in a morter with ayrenn rawe do þerto suger, salt, raysouns coraunce, dates mynced, and powdour of Peper powdour gylofre. an do it in a bladder, and lat it seeþ til it be ynowhz. and whan it is ynowh, kerf it leshe it [2] in likenesse of a peskodde [3], and take grete raysouns and grynde hem in a morter, drawe hem Up wiþ rede wyne, do þerto mylke of almaundes colour it with saunders an safroun.

and do þerto powdour of peper an of gilofre and boile it. and whan it is iboiled; take powdour of canel and gynger, and temper it up with wyne. and do alle þise thynges togyder. and loke þat it be rennyns [4], and lat it not seeþ after that it is cast togyder, an serue it forth.

[1] Leche Lumbard. So called from the country. Randle Home says, *Leach* is "a kind of jelly made of cream, ising-glass, sugar and almonds, with other compounds." [2] Leshe it. Vide Gloss. [3] Peskodde. Hull or pod of a pea. [4] rennyns. Perhaps *thin,* from the old *renne,* to run. Vide Gloss.

CONNYNGES IN CLERE BROTH. XX.III. VI.

Take Connynges and smyte hem in gobetes and waissh hem and do hem in feyre water and wyne, and seeþ hem and skym hem. and whan þey buth isode pyke hem clene, and drawe the broth thurgh a straynour and do the flessh þerwith in a Possynet and styne it [1]. and do þerto vynegur and powdour or gynger and a grete quantite and salt after the last boillyng and serue it forth.

[1] styne it. Close it. V. Gloss.

PAYN RAGOUN [1]. XX.III. VII.

Take hony suger and clarifie it togydre. and boile it with esy fyre, and kepe it wel fro brennyng and whan it hath yboiled a while; take up a drope [2] þerof wiþ þy fyngur and do it in a litel water and loke if it hong [3] togydre. and take it fro the fyre and do þerto the thriddendele [4] an powdour gyngener and stere [5] it togyder til it bigynne to thik and cast it on a wete [6] table. lesh it and serue it forth with fryed mete on flessh dayes or on fysshe dayes.

[1] Payn ragoun. It is not at all explained in the Recipe. [2] Drope. Drop. [3] hong. Hing, or hang. [4] thriddendele. Third part, perhaps, *ofbr ede*, i. e. of bread, may be casually omitted here. V. Gloss. [5] stere. stir. [6] wete. wet.

LETE LARDES [1]. XX.III. VIII.

Take parsel and grynde with a Cowe mylk, medle it with ayrenn and

lard ydyced take mylke after þat þou hast to done [2] and myng [3] þerwith. and make þerof dyuerse colours. If þou wolt have zelow, do þerto safroun and no parsel. If þou wolt have it white; nonþer parsel ne safroun but do þerto amydoun. If þou wilt have rede do þerto sandres. If þou wilt have pownas [4] do þerto turnesole [5]. If þou wilt have blak do þerto blode ysode and fryed. and set on the fyre in as many vessels as þou hast colours þerto and seeþ it wel and lay þise colours in a cloth first oon. and sithen anoþer upon him. and sithen the þridde and the ferthe. and presse it harde til it be all out clene. And whan it is al colde, lesh it thynne, put it in a panne and fry it wel. and serue it forth.

[1] Lete Lardes. *Lards* in form of Dice are noticed in the process.
See Lel. Coll. VI. p. 5. *Lete* is the Fr. *Lait*, milk. V. No. 81.
or Brit. *Llaeth*. Hence, perhaps, *LetheCpyrus* and *LetheRube*.
Lel. Coll. IV. p. 227. But VI. p. 5, it is *Leche*.

[2] to done, i. e. done.

[3] myng. mix.

[4] pownas. Qu.

[5] turnesole. Not the flower *Heliotrope*, but a drug. Northumb.
Book, p. 3. 19. I suppose it to be *Turmeric*. V. Brooke's Nat. Hist.
of Vegetables, p. 9. where it is used both in victuals and for dying.

FURMENTE WITH PORPAYS [1]. XX.III. IX.

Take Almandes blanched. bray hem and drawe hem up with faire water, make furmente as before [2] and cast þer furmente þerto. & messe it with Porpays.

[1] Porpays. *Porpeys*, Contents, and so No. 116. Porpus. [2] as before. This is the first mention of it.

PERREY OF PESOUN [1]. XX.III. X.

Take pesoun and seeþ hem fast and covere hem til þei berst. þenne take up hem and cole hem thurgh a cloth. take oynouns and mynce hem and seeþ hem in the same sewe and oile þerwith, cast þerto sugur, salt and safroun, and seeþ hem wel þeratt þerafter and serue hem forth.

[1] Perrey of Pesoun, i.e. Peas. *Perrey* seems to mean pulp: vide No. 73. Mr. Ozell in Rabelais, IV. c. 60. renders *Pureedepois* by *Peassoup*.

PESON OF ALMAYNE [1]. XX.III. XI

Take white pesoun, waisshe hem seeþ hem a grete while, take hem and cole hem thurgh a cloth, waisshe hem in colde water til the hulles go off, cast hem in a pot and couere þat no breth [2] go out. and boile hem right wel. and cast þerinne gode mylke of allmandes and a pertye of flour of Rys wiþ powdour gynger safroun. and salt.

[1] Almayne. Germany; called Almony No. 47. [2] breth. Breath, air, steam. Ms. Ed. No. 2.

CHYCHES [1]. XX.III. XII.

Take chiches and wry hem [2] in ashes all nyzt, oþer lay hem in hoot aymers [3], at morrowe [4], waisshe hem in clene water and do hem ouer the fire with clene water. seeþ hem up and do þerto oyle, garlec, hole safroun. powdour fort and salt, seeþ it and messe it forth.

[1] Chyches. *Viciæ*, vetches. In Fr. *Chiches*. [2] Wry hem. *Dry hem*, or *coverhem* . Chaucer, v. wrey. [3] Aymers. Embers; of which it is evidently a corruption. [4] at morrowe. Next Morning.

FRENCHE [1]. XX.III. XIII.

Take and seeþ white peson and take oute þe perrey [2] & parboile erbis & hewe hem grete & cast hem in a pot with the perrey pulle oynouns & seeþ hem hole wel in water & do hem to þe Perrey with oile & salt, colour it with safroun & messe it and cast þeron powdour douce.

[1] Frenche. Contents have it more fully, *FrencheOwtes* . V. ad No. 6. [2] Perrey. Pulp. V. ad No. 70.

MAKKE [1]. XX.III. XIIII.

Take drawen benes and seeþ hem wel. take hem up of the water and cast hem in a morter grynde hem al to doust til þei be white as eny mylk, chawf [2] a litell rede wyne, cast þeramong in þe gryndyng, do þerto salt, leshe it in disshes. þanne take Oynouns and mynce hem smale and seeþ hem in oile til þey be al broun [3]. and florissh the disshes therwith. and serue it forth.

[1] Makke. *Ignotum.* [2] Chawf. Warm. [3] broun. Brown.

AQUAPATYS [1]. XX.III. XV.

Pill garlec and cast it in a pot with water and oile. and seeþ it, do þerto safroun, salt, and powdour fort and dresse it forth hool.

[1] Aquapatys. *Aquapates,* Contents. Perhaps named from the water used in it.

SALAT. XX.III. XVI.

Take persel, sawge, garlec, chibolles, oynouns, leek, borage, myntes, porrectes [1], fenel and ton tressis [2], rew, rosemarye, purslarye [3], laue and waische hem clene, pike hem, pluk hem small wiþ þyn [4] honde and myng hem wel with rawe oile. lay on vynegur and salt, and serue it forth.

[1] Porrectes. Fr. *Porrette.* [2] Ton tressis. Cresses. V. Gloss. [3] Purslarye. Purslain. [4] þyn. thine.

FENKEL IN SOPPES. XX.III. XVII.

Take blades of Fenkel. shrede hem not to smale, do hem to seeþ in water and oile and oynouns mynced þerwith. do þerto safroun and salt and powdour douce, serue it forth, take brede ytosted and lay the sewe onoward.

CLAT [1]. XX.III. XVIII.

Take elena campana and seeþ it water [2]. take it up and grynde it wel in a morter. temper it up with ayrenn safroun and salt and do it ouer the fire and lat it not boile. cast above powdour douce and serue it forth.

[1] Clat. Qu. [2] water; r. *inwater* , as in No. 79.

APPULMOY [1]. XX.III. XIX.

Take Apples and seeþ hem in water, drawe hem thurgh a straynour. take almaunde mylke & hony and flour of Rys, safroun and powdour fort and salt. and seeþ it stondyng [2].

[1] Appulmoy. *Appulmos.* Ms. Ed. No. 17. named from the apples employed. V. No. 149. [2] stondyng. thick.

SLETE [1] SOPPES. XX.IIII.

Take white of Lekes and slyt hem, and do hem to seeþ in wyne, oile and salt, rost brede and lay in dysshes and the sewe above and serue it forth.

[1] Slete. slit.

LETELORYE [1]. XX.IIII. I.

Take Ayrenn and wryng hem thurgh a styunour and do þerto cowe mylke with butter and safroun and salt and seeþ it wel. leshe it. and loke þat it be stondyng. and serue it forth.

[1] Letelorye. The latter part of the compound is unknown, the first is Fr. *Lait*, milk. Vide No. 68.

SOWPES DORRY [1]. XX.IIII. II.

Take Almaundes brayed, drawe hem up with wyne. ooile it, cast þeruppon safroun and salt, take brede itosted in wyne. lay þerof a leyne [2] and anoþer of þe sewe and alle togydre. florish it with sugur powdour gyngur and serue it forth.

[1] Sowpes Dorry. Sops endorsed. V. *Dorry* in Gloss. [2] A leyne. a layer.

RAPE [1]. XX.IIII. III.

Take half fyges and half raisouns pike hem and waisshe

hem in water skalde hem in wyne. bray hem in a morter, and drawe hem thurgh a straynour. cast hem in a pot and þerwiþ powdour of peper and ooþer good powdours. alay it up with flour of Rys. and colour it with saundres. salt it. & messe it forth.

[1] Rape. A dissyllable, as appears from *Rapey* in the Contents. *Rapy*, Ms. Ed. No. 49. *Rapee*, ibid. II. 28.

SAWSE SARZYNE [1]. XX.IIII. IIII.

Take heppes and make hem clene. take Almaundes blaunched, frye hem in oile and bray hem in a morter with heppes. drawe it up with rede wyne, and do þerin sugur ynowhz with Powdour fort, lat it be stondyng, and alay it with flour of Rys. and colour it with alkenet and messe it forth. and florish it with Pomme garnet. If þou wilt in flesshe day. seeþ Capouns and take the brawnn and tese hem smal and do þerto. and make the lico [2] of þis broth.

> [1] Sawse Sarzyne. *Sause*. Contents. *Saracen*, we presume, from the nation or people. There is a Recipe in Ms. Ed. No. 54 for a Bruet of *Sarcynesse*, but there are no pomgranates concerned.

[2] lico. liquor.

CRÈME OF ALMAUNDES. XX.IIII. V.

Take Almaundes blaunched, grynde hem and drawe hem up thykke, set hem ouer the fyre & boile hem. set hem adoun and spryng [1] hem wicii Vyneger, cast hem abrode uppon a cloth and cast uppon hem sugur. whan it is colde gadre it togydre and leshe it in dysshes.

> [1] spryng. sprinkle.

GREWEL OF ALMAUNDES. XX.IIII. VI.

Take Almaundes blaunched, bray hem with oot meel [1]. and draw hem up with water. cast þeron Safroun & salt &c.

> [1] oot meel. oat-meal.

CAWDEL OF ALMAUND MYLK. XX.IIII. VII.

Take Almaundes blaunched and drawe hem up with wyne, do þerto powdour of gyngur and sugur and colour it with Safroun. boile it and serue it forth.

JOWTES [1] OF ALMAUND MYLKE. XX.IIII. VIII.

Take erbes, boile hem, hewe hem and grynde hem smale. and drawe hem up with water. set hem on the fire and seeþ the rowtes with the mylke. and cast þeron sugur & salt. & serue it forth.

[1] Jowtes. V. ad No. 60.

FYGEY [1]. XX.IIII. IX.

Take Almaundes blanched, grynde hem and drawe hem up with water and wyne: quarter fygur hole raisouns. cast þerto powdour gyngur and hony clarified. seeþ it wel & salt it, and serue forth.

[1] Fygey. So named from the figs therein used. A different Recipe, Ms. Ed. No. 3, has no figs.

POCHEE [1]. XX.IIII. X.

Take Ayrenn and breke hem in scaldyng hoot water. and whan þei bene sode ynowh. take hem up and take zolkes of ayren and rawe mylke and swyng hem togydre, and do þerto powdour gyngur safroun and salt, set it ouere the fire, and lat it not boile, and take ayrenn isode & cast þe sew onoward. & serue it forth.

[1] Pochee. Poached eggs. Very different from the present way.

BREWET OF AYRENN. XX.IIII. XI.

Take ayrenn, water and butter, and seeþ hem yfere with safroun and gobettes of chese. wryng ayrenn thurgh a straynour. whan the water hath soden awhile: take þenne the ayrenn and swyng hem with verious. and cast þerto. set it ouere the fire and lat it not boile. and serue it forth.

MACROWS [1]. XX.IIII. XII.

Take and make a thynne foyle of dowh. and kerve it on peces, and cast hem on boillyng water & seeþ it wele. take chese and grate it and butter cast bynethen and above as losyns. and serue forth.

[1] Macrows. *Maccherone*, according to the Recipe in *Altieri*, corresponds nearly enough with our process; so that this title seems to want mending, and yet I know not how to do it to satisfaction.

TOSTEE [1]. XX.IIII. XIII.

Take wyne and hony and found it [2] togyder and skym it clene. and seeþ it long, do þerto powdour of gyngur. peper and salt, tost brede and lay the sew þerto. kerue pecys of gyngur and flour it þerwith and messe it forth.

[1] Tostee. So called from the toasted bread. [2] found it. mix it.

GYNGAWDRY [1]. XX.IIII. XIIII.

Take the Powche [2] and the Lyuour [3] of haddok, codlyng and hake [4] and of ooþer fisshe, parboile hem, take hem and dyce hem small, take of the self broth and wyne, a layour of brede of galyntyne with gode powdours and salt, cast þat fysshe þerinne and boile it. & do þerto amydoun. & colour it grene.

[1] Gyngawdry. Qu. [2] Powche. Crop or stomach. [3] Lyuour. Liver. V. No. 137. [4] Hake. "Asellus alter, sive Merlucius, Aldrov." So Mr. Ray. See Pennant, III. p. 156.

ERBOWLE [1]. XX.IIII. XV.

Take bolas and scald hem with wyne and drawe hem with [2] a straynour do hem in a pot, clarify hony and do þerto with powdour fort. and flour of Rys. Salt it & florish it with whyte aneys. & serue it forth.

[1] Erbowle. Perhaps from the *Belas*, or Bullace employed. [2] with, i.e. thurgh or thorough.

RESMOLLE [1]. XX.IIII. XVI.

Take Almaundes blaunched and drawe hem up with water and alye it with flour of Rys and do þerto powdour of gyngur sugur and salt, and loke it be not stondyng [2], messe it and serue it forth.

[1] Resmolle. From the Rice there used; for Ms. Ed. II. No. 5. has *Rysmoyle*, where *moyle* seems to be Fr. *moile*, as written also in the Roll. *Ricemolenspotage* . Lel. Coll. VI. p. 26.
[2] Not stondyng. Thin, diluted. V. No. 98. Not to [too] stondyng, 121.

VYAUNDE CYPRE [1]. XX.IIII. XVII.

Take oot mele and pike out the stones and grynde hem smal, and drawe hem thurgh a straynour. take mede oþer wyne ifonded in sugur and do þise þerinne. do þerto powdour and salt, and alay it with flour of Rys and do þat it be stondyng. if thou wilt on flesh day; take hennes and pork ysode & grynde hem smale and do þerto. & messe it forth.

[1] Cypre. *Cipre*, Contents here and No. 98.

VYANDE CYPRE OF SAMOUN [1]. XX.IIII. XVIII.

Take Almandes and bray hem unblaunched. take calwar [2] Samoun and seeþ it in lewe water [3] drawe up þyn Almandes with the broth. pyke out the bones out of the fyssh clene & grynde it small & cast þy mylk & þat togyder & alye it with flour of Rys, do þerto powdour fort, sugur & salt & colour it with alkenet & loke þat hit be not stondyng and messe it forth.

[1] Samoun. Salmon.
[2] calwar. Salwar, No. 167. R. Holme says, "*Calver* is a term used to a Flounder when to be boiled in oil, vinegar, and spices and to be kept in it." But in Lancashire Salmon newly taken and immediately dressed is called *CalverSalmon* : and in Littleton *Salar* is a young salmon.
[3] lewe water. warm. V. Gloss.

VYANND RYAL. XX.IIII. XIX.

Take wyne greke, oþer rynysshe wyne and hony clarified þerwith. take flour of rys powdour of Gyngur oþ of peper & canel. oþer flour of canel. powdour of clowes, safroun. sugur cypre. mylberyes, oþer saundres. & medle alle þise togider. boile it and salt it. and loke þat it be stondyng.

COMPOST [1]. C.

Take rote of parsel. pasternak of rasenns [2]. scrape hem waisthe hem clene. take rapes & caboches ypared and icorne [3]. take an erthen panne with clene water & set it on the fire. cast all þise þerinne. whan þey buth boiled cast þerto peeres & parboile hem wel. take þise thynges up & lat it kele on a fair cloth, do þerto salt whan it is colde in a vessel take vineger & powdour & safroun & do þerto. & lat alle þise thinges lye þerin al nyzt oþer al day, take wyne greke and hony clarified togider lumbarde mustard & raisouns corance al hool. & grynde powdour of canel powdour douce. & aneys hole. & fenell seed. take alle þise thynges & cast togyder in a pot of erthe. and take þerof whan þou wilt & serue forth.

[1] Compost. A composition to be always ready at hand. Holme, III. p. 78. Lel. Coll. VI. p. 5. [2] Pasternak of rasenns. Qu. [3] ypared and icorne. The first relates to the Rapes, the second to the Caboches, and means carved or cut in pieces.

GELE [1] OF FYSSH. C. I.

Take Tenches, pykes [2], eelys, turbut and plays [3], kerue hem to pecys. scalde hem & waische hem clene. drye hem with a cloth do hem in a panne do þerto half vyneger & half wyne & seeþ it wel. & take the Fysshe and pike it clene, cole the broth thurgh a cloth into a erthen panne. do þerto powdour of pep and safroun ynowh. lat it seeþ and skym it wel whan it is ysode dof [4] grees clene, cowche fisshes on chargeours & cole the sewe thorow a cloth onoward & serue it forth.

[1] Gele. Jelly. *Gelee*, Contents here and in the next Recipe.
Gely, Ms. Ed. No. 55, which presents us with much the same prescription.

[2] It is commonly thought this fish was not extant in England till the reign of H. VIII.; but see No. 107. 109. 114. So Lucys, or Tenchis, Ms. Ed. II 1. 3. Pygus or Tenchis, II. 2. Pikys, 33 Chaucer, v. Luce; and Lel. Coll. IV. p. 226. VI. p. 1. 5. *Lucesalt*. Ibid. p. 6. Mr. Topham's Ms. written about 1230, mentions *Luposaquaticosfive Luceas* amongst the fish which the fishmonger was to have in his shop. They were the arms of the Lucy family so early as Edw. I. See also Pennant's Zool. III. p. 280, 410.

[3] Plays. Plaise, the fish.

[4] Dof, i. e. do of.

GELE OF FLESSH. C. II.

Take swyner feet & snowter and the eerys [1]. capouns. connynges calues fete. & wiasche hem clene. & do hem to seeþ in the þriddel [2] of wyne & vyneger and water and make forth as bifore.

[1] Eerys. Ears. [2] Thriddel. V. ad No. 67.

CHYSANNE [1]. C. III.

Take Roches. hole Tenches and plays & sinyte hem to gobettes. fry hem in oyle blaunche almaundes. fry hem & cast wyne & of vyneger þer pridde part þerwith fyges drawen & do þerto powdour fort and salt. boile it. lay the Fisshe in an erthen panne cast the sewe þerto. seeþ oynouns ymynced & cast þerinne. kepe hit and ete it colde.

[1] Chysanne. Qu.

CONGUR [1] IN SAWSE. C. IIII.

Take the Conger and scald hym. and smyte hym in pecys & seeþ hym. take parsel. mynt. peleter. rosmarye. & a litul sawge. brede and salt, powdour fort and a litel garlec, clower a lite, take and grynd it wel, drawe it up with vyneger thurgh a clot. cast the fyssh in a vessel and do þe sewe onoward & serue it forth.

[1] Congur. The Eel called *Congre. Sawce*, Contents here, and No. 105, 106.

RYGH [1] IN SAWSE. C. V.

Take Ryghzes and make hem clene and do hem to seeþ, pyke hem clene and frye hem in oile. take Almandes and grynde hem in water or wyne, do þerto almandes blaunched hole fryed in oile. & coraunce seeþ the lyour grynde it smale & do þerto garlec ygronde & litel salt & verious powdour fort & safroun & boile it yfere, lay the Fysshe in a vessel and cast the sewe þerto. and messe it forth colde.

[1] Rygh. A Fish, and probably the *Ruffe*.

MAKEREL IN SAWSE. C. VI.

Take Makerels and smyte hem on pecys. cast hem on water and various. seeþ hem with mynter and wiþ oother erbes, colour it grene or zelow, and messe it forth.

PYKES IN BRASEY [1]. C. VII.

Take Pykes and undo hem on þe wombes [2] and waisshe hem clene and lay hem on a roost Irne [3] þenne take gode wyne and powdour gynger & sugur good wone [4] & salt, and boile it in an erthen panne & messe forth þe pyke & lay the sewe onoward.

[1] Brasey. Qu. [2] Wombs. bellies. [3] roost Irene. a roasting iron. [4] good wone. a good deal. V. Gloss.

PORPEYS IN BROTH. C. VIII.

Make as þou madest Noumbles of Flesh with oynouns.

BALLOC [1] BROTH. C. IX.

Take Eelys and hilde [2] hem and kerue hem to pecys and do hem to seeþ in water and wyne so þat it be a litel ouer stepid [3]. do þerto sawge and ooþer erbis with few [4] oynouns ymynced, whan the Eelis buth soden ynowz do hem in a vessel, take a pyke and kerue it to gobettes and seeþ hym in the same broth do þerto powdour gynger galyngale canel and peper, salt it and cast the Eelys þerto & messe it forth.

[1] Balloc. *Ballok*, Contents. [2] hilde. skin. [3] on stepid. steeped therein. V. No. 110. [4] few, i.e. a few.

ELES IN BREWET. C. X.

Take Crustes of brede and wyne and make a lyour, do þerto oynouns ymynced, powdour. & canel. & a litel water and wyne. loke þat it be stepid, do þerto salt, kerue þin Eelis & seeþ hem wel and serue hem forth.

[1] shell, take of the shells. [2] hare. their. *her*. No. 123. Chaucer.

MUSKELS [1] IN BREWET. XX.VI. II.

Take muskels, pyke hem, seeþ hem with the owne broth, make a lyour of crustes [2] & vynegur do in oynouns mynced. & cast the muskels þerto & seeþ it. & do þerto powdour with a lytel salt & safron the samewise make of oysters.

[1] Muskles. *muskels* below, and the Contents. Muscles. [2] crustes. i.e. of bread.

OYSTERS IN CYNEE. XX.VI. III.

Take Oysters parboile hem in her owne broth, make a lyour of crustes

of brede & drawe it up wiþ the broth and vynegur mynce oynouns & do þerto with erbes. & cast the oysters þerinne. boile it. & do þerto powdour fort & salt. & messe it forth.

CAWDEL OF MUSKELS. XX.VI. IIII.

Take and seeþ muskels, pyke hem clene, and waisshe hem clene in wyne. take almandes & bray hem. take somme of the muskels and grynde hem. & some hewe smale, drawe the muskels yground with the self broth. wryng the almaundes with faire water. do alle þise togider. do þerto verious and vyneger. take whyte of lekes & parboile hem wel. wryng oute the water and hewe hem smale. cast oile þerto with oynouns parboiled & mynced smale do þerto powdour fort, safroun and salt. a lytel seeþ it not to to [1] stondyng & messe it forth.

[1] to to, i. e. too too. Vide No. 17.

MORTREWS OF FYSSH. XX.VI. V.

Take codlyng, haddok, oþ hake and lynours with the rawnes [1] and seeþ it wel in water. pyke out þe bones, grynde smale the Fysshe, drawe a lyour of almaundes & brede with the self broth. and do the Fysshe grounden þerto. and seeþ it and do þerto powdour fort, safroun and salt, and make it stondyng.

[1] rawnes. roes.

LAUMPREYS IN GALYNTYNE. XX.VI. VI.

Take Laumpreys and sle [1] hem with vynegur oþer with white wyne & salt, scalde hem in water. slyt hem a litel at þer nauel…. & rest a litel at the nauel. take out the guttes at the ende. kepe wele the blode. put the Laumprey on a spyt. roost hym & kepe wel the grece. grynde raysouns of coraunce. hym up [2] with vyneger. wyne. and crustes of brede. do þerto powdour of gyngur. of galyngale [3]. flour of canel. powdour of clowes, and do þerto raisouns of coraunce hoole. with þe blode & þe grece. seeþ it & salt it, boile it not to stondyng, take up the Laumprey do hym in a chargeour [4], & lay þe sewe onoward, & serue hym forth.

[1] sle. slay, kill. [2] hym up. A word seems omitted; *drawe* or *lye*. [3] of galyngale, i. e. powder. V. No. 101. [4] Chargeour. charger or dish. V. No. 127.

LAUMPROUNS IN GALYNTYNE. XX.VI. VII.

Take Lamprouns and scalde hem. seeþ hem, meng powdour galyngale and some of the broth togyder & boile it & do þerto powdour of gyngur & salt. take the Laumprouns & boile hem & lay hem in dysshes. & lay the sewe above. & serue fort.

LOSEYNS [1] IN FYSSH DAY. XX.VI. VIII.

Take Almandes unblaunched and waisthe hem clene, drawe hem up with water. seeþ þe mylke & alye it up with loseyns. cast þerto safroun. sugur. & salt & messe it forth with colyandre in confyt rede, & serue it forth.

    [1] Loseyns. *Losyns*, Contents.

SOWPER OF GALYNTYNE [1]. XX.VI. IX.

Take powdour of galyngale with sugur and salt and boile it yfere. take brede ytosted. and lay the sewe onoward. and serue it forth.

    [1] Sowpes of Galyntyne. Contents has *in*, recte. *Sowpes* means Sops.

SOBRE SAWSE. XX.VI. X.

Take Raysouns, grynde hem with crustes of brede; and drawe it up with wyne. do þerto gode powdours and salt. and seeþ it. fry roches, looches, sool, oþer ooþer gode Fyssh, cast þe sewe above, & serue it forth.

COLD BREWET. XX.VI. XI.

Take crome [1] of almaundes. dry it in a cloth. and whan it is dryed do it in a vessel, do þerto salt, sugur, and white powdour of gyngur and Juys of Fenel and wyne. and lat it wel stonde. lay full & messe & dresse it forth.

[1] crome. crumb, pulp.

PEERES [1] IN CONFYT. XX.VI. XII.

Take peeres and pare hem clene. take gode rede wyne & mulberes [2] oþer saundres and seeþ þe peeres þerin & whan þei buth ysode, take hem up, make a syryp of wyne greke. oþer vernage [3] with blaunche powdour oþer white sugur and powdour gyngur & do the peres þerin. seeþ it a lytel & messe it forth.

[1] Peeres. pears. [2] mulberes. mulberries, for colouring. [3] Vernage. Vernaccia, a sort of Italian white wine. V. Gloss.

EGURDOUCE [1] OF FYSSHE. XX.VI. XIII.

Take Loches oþer Tenches oþer Solys smyte hem on pecys. fry hem in oyle. take half wyne half vynegur and sugur & make a siryp. do þerto oynouns icorue [2] raisouns coraunce. and grete raysouns. do þerto hole spices. gode powdours and salt. messe þe fyssh & lay þe sewe aboue and serue forth.

[1] Egurdouce. Vide Gloss. [2] icorue, icorven. cut. V. Gloss.

COLDE BREWET. XX.VI. XIIII.

Take Almaundes and grynde hem. take the tweydel [1] of wyne oþer the þriddell of vynegur. drawe up the Almaundes þerwith. take anys sugur & branches of fenel grene a fewe. & drawe hem up togyder with þer mylke take poudour of canell. of gyngur. clowes. & maces hoole. take kydde oþer chikenns oþer flessh. & choppe hem small and seeþ hem. take all þis flessh whan it is sodenn & lay it in a clene vessel & boile þer sewe & cast þerto salt. þenne cast al þis in þe pot with flesh. &ter. [2]

[1] Tweydel. Two parts. [2] &ter. i. e. serue forth.

PEVORAT [1] FOR VEEL AND VENYSOUN. XX.VI. XV.

Take Brede & fry it in grece. drawe it up with broth and vynegur, take þerto powdour of peper & salt and sette it on the fyre. boile it and messe it forth.

[1] Pevorat. Peverade, from the pepper of which it is principally composed.

SAWSE [2] BLAUNCHE FOR CAPOUNS YSODE. XX.VI. XVI.

Take Almandes blaunched and grynd hem al to doust. temper it up with verions and powdour or gyngyner and messe it forth.

[2] Sawse. *Sawce*, Contents. As No. 137.

SAWSE NOYRE FOR CAPOUNS YROSTED. XX.VI. XVII.

Take the lyuer of Capons and roost it wel. take anyse and greynes de Parys [1]. gyngur. canel. & a lytill crust of brede and grinde it smale. and grynde it up with verions. and witþ grece of Capouns. boyle it and serue it forth.

[1] de Parys. Of Paradise. V. Pref.

GALYNTYNE [1]. XX.VI. XVIII.

Take crustes of Brede and grynde hem smale, do þerto powdour of galyngale, of canel, of gyngyner and salt it, tempre it with vynegur and drawe it up þurgh a straynour & messe it forth.

[1] Galyntyne. Galentyne, Contents.

GYNGENER [1]. XX.VI. XIX.

Take payndemayn and pare it clene and funde it in Vinegur, grynde it and temper it wiþ Vynegur, and with powdour gyngur and salt, drawe it thurgh a straynour. and serue forth.

[1] Gyngener. From the powder of Ginger therein used.

VERDE [1] SAWSE. XX.VII.

Take parsel. mynt. garlek. a litul serpell [2] and sawge, a litul canel. gyngur. piper. wyne. brede. vynegur & salt grynde it smal with

safroun & messe it forth.

[1] Verde. It has the sound of *Green-sauce*, but as there is no Sorel in it, it is so named from the other herbs. [2] a litul serpell. Wild thyme.

SAWSE NOYRE FOR MALARD. XX.VII. I.

Take brede and blode iboiled. and grynde it and drawe it thurgh a cloth with Vynegur, do þerto powdour of gyngur ad of peper. & þe grece of the Maulard. salt it. boile it wel and serue it forth.

CAWDEL FOR GEES. XX.VII. II.

Take garlec and grynde it smale. Safroun and flour þerwith & salt. and temper it up with Cowe Mylke. and seeþ it wel and serue it forth.

CHAWDOUN [1] FOR SWANNES XX.VII. III.

Take þe lyuer and þe offall [2] of the Swannes & do it to seeþ in gode broth. take it up. take out þe bonys. take & hewe the flessh smale. make a Lyour of crustes of brede & of þe blode of þe Swan ysoden. & do þerto powdour of clowes & of piper & of wyne & salt, & seeþ it & cast þe flessh þerto ihewed. and messe it forth with þe Swan.

[1] Chawdoun. V. Gloss. [2] offall. *Exta*, Gibles.

SAWSE CAMELYNE [1]. XX.VII. IIII.

Take Raysouns of Coraunce. & kyrnels of notys. & crustes of brede & powdour of gyngur clowes flour of canel. bray it [2] wel togyder and do it þerto. salt it, temper it up with vynegur. and serue it forth.

[1] Camelyne. Qu. if *Canelyne* from the *Fluor of Canel*? [2] bray. bray.

LUMBARD MUSTARD. XX.VII. V.

Take Mustard seed and waishe it & drye it in an ovene, grynde it drye. farse it thurgh a farse. clarifie hony with wyne & vynegur & stere it wel togedrer and make it thikke ynowz. & whan þou wilt spende þerof make it tnynne with wyne.

NOTA. XX.VII. VI.

Cranes [1] and Herouns shul be armed [2] with lardes of Swyne. and eten with gyngur.

> [1] Cranes. A dish frequent formerly at great tables. Archæologia,
> II. p. 171. mentioned with Herons, as here, Ms. Ed. 3. where the same
> Recipe occurs. et v. Lel. Coll. IV. p. 226. VI. p. 38. Rabelais, IV.
> c. 59. E. of Devon's Feast.
> [2] armed. Ms. Ed. No. 3. has *enarmed*, as may be read there.
> *Enarmed*, however, in Lel. Collect. IV. p. 225. means, decorated
> with coate of arms. Sheldes of Brawn are there *in armor*, p. 226.
> However, there is such a word as *enorned*. Leland, p. 280. 285. 297.
> which approaches nearer.

NOTA. XX.VII. VII.

Pokok and Partruch shul be parboiled. lardid and rosted. and eten with gyngeuer.

FRY BLAUNCHED. XX.VII. VIII.

Take Almandes blaunched and grynde hem al to doust, do þise in a thynne foile. close it þerinnne fast. and fry it in Oile. clarifie hony with Wyne. & bake it þerwith.

FRYTOUR OF PASTERNAKES OF APPLES [1]. XX.VII. IX.

Take skyrwater and pasternakes and apples, & parboile hem, make a batour of flour and ayrenn, cast þerto ale. safroun & salt. wete hem in þe batour and frye hem in oile or in grece. do þerto Almaund Mylk. & serue it forth.

[1] Frytour, &c. Contents has only, *Frytours of Pasternakes*. N. B. *Frytour* is *Fritter*.

FRYTOUR OF MYLKE. XX.VII. X.

Take of cruddes [1] and presse out þe wheyze [2]. do þerto sum whyte of ayrenn. fry hem. do þerto. & lay on sugur and messe forth.

[1] Cruddes. Curds, per metathesin. [2] wheyze. whey.

FRYTOUR OF ERBES. XX.VII. XI.

Take gode erbys. grynde hem and medle [1] hem with flour and water & a lytel zest and salt, and frye hem in oyle. and ete hem with clere hony.

[1] medle. mix.

RASYOLS [1]. XX.VII. XII.

Take swyne lyuoers and seeþ hem wel. take brede & grate it. and take zolkes of ayrenn. & make hit sowple [2] and do þerto a lytull of lard carnoun lyche a dee [3]. chese gratyd [4] & whyte grece. powdour douce & of gyngur & wynde it to balles [5] as grete as apples. take þe calle of þe swyne & cast euere [6] by hym self þerin. Make a Crust in a trape [7]. and lay þe ball þerin & bake it. and whan þey buth ynowz: put þerin a layour of ayrenn with powdour fort and Safroun. and serue it forth.

[1] Rasyols. Rasiowls, Contents. Qu. the etymen. [2] sowple. supple. [3] carnoun lyche a dee. Cut like dice, diced. Fr. *De*; singular of *Dice*. [4] gratyd. grated. *igrated*, No. 153. [5] wynde it to balles, make it into Balls. [6] euere. each. [7] trape. pan, or dish. French.

WHYTE MYLATES [1]. XX.VII. XIII.

Take Ayrenn and wryng hem thurgh a cloth. take powdour fort, brede igrated, & safroun, & cast þerto a gode quantite of vynegur with a litull salt, medle all yfere. make a foile in a trape & bake it wel þerinne. and serue it forth.

    [1] Mylates. Contents, *Milates*; but 155 as here. Qu.

CRUSTARDES [1] OF FLESSH. XX.VII. XIIII.

Take peiouns [2], chykens, and smale briddes smyte hem in gobettes. & seeþ hem alle ifere in god broþ wiþ veriaws [3] do þerto safroun, make a crust in a trape. and pynche it. & cowche þe flessh þerinne. & cast þerinne Raisouns coraunce. powdour douce and salt. breke ayrenn and wryng hem thurgh a cloth & swyng þe sewe of þe stewe þerwith and helde it [4] uppon the flessh. couere it & bake it wel. and serue it forth.

    [1] Crustards. Pies. [2] peiouns. pigeons. V. ad No. 48. [3] veriaws. Verjuice. [4] helde it. pour, cast.

MYLATES OF PORK. XX.VII. XV.

Hewe Pork al to pecys and medle it with ayrenn & chese igrated. do þerto powdour fort safroun & pyneres [1] with salt, make a crust in a trape, bake it wel þerinne, and serue it forth.

    [1] pyneres. Vide Pref.

CRUSTARDES OF FYSSHE. XX.VII. XVI.

Take loches, laumprouns, and Eelis. smyte hem on pecys, and stewe hem wiþ Almaund Mylke and verions, frye the loches in oile as tofore. and lay þe fissh þerinne. cast þeron powdour fort powdour douce. with raysons coraunce & prunes damysyns. take galyntyn and þe sewe þerinne, and swyng it togyder and cast in the trape. & bake it and serue it forth.

CRUSTARDES OF EERBIS [1] ON FYSSH DAY. XX.VII. XVII.

Take gode Eerbys and grynde hem smale with wallenotes pyked clene. a grete portioun. lye it up almost wiþ as myche verions as water. seeþ it wel with powdour and Safroun withoute Salt. make a crust in a trape and do þe fyssh þerinne unstewed wiþ a litel oile & gode Powdour. whan it is half ybake do þe sewe þerto & bake it up. If þou wilt make it clere of Fyssh seeþ ayrenn harde. & take out þe zolkes & grinde hem with gode powdours. and alye it up with gode stewes [2] and serue it forth.

   [1] Erbis. Rather *Erbis and Fissh*. [2] stewes. V. No. 170.

LESSHES [1] FRYED IN LENTON [2]. XX.VII. XVIII.

Drawe a thick almaunde Mylke wiþ water. take dates and pyke hem clene with apples and peeres & mynce hem with prunes damysyns. take out þe stones out of þe prunes. & kerue the prunes a two. do þerto Raisouns sugur. flour of canel. hoole macys and clowes. gode powdours & salt. colour hem up with saundres. meng þise with oile, make a coffyn as þou didest bifore & do þis Fars [3] þerin. and bake it wel and serue it forth.

   [1] Leshes. V. Leche Lumbard in Gloss. [2] lenton. Lentoun, Contents, i. e. Lent. [3] Fars. Vide Gloss.

WASTELS YFARCED. XX.VII. XIX.

Take a Wastel and hewe out þe crummes. take ayrenn & shepis talow & þe crummes of þe same Wastell powdour fort & salt with Safroun and Raisouns coraunce. & medle alle þise yfere & do it in þe Wastel. close it & bynde it fast togidre. and seeþ it wel.

SAWGE YFARCED. XX.VIII.

Take sawge. grynde it and temper it up with ayrenn. a saweyster [1] & kerf hym to gobettes and cast it in a possynet. and do þerwiþ grece & frye it. Whan it is fryed ynowz cast þerto sawge with ayren make it not to harde. cast þerto powdour douce, messe it forth. If it be in Ymber day; take sauge butter & ayrenn. and lat it stonde wel by þe sause [2], & serue it forth.

    [1] saweyster. Qu. [2] stonde wel by the sause. Become thick with the sawce.

SAWGEAT [1]. XX.VIII. I.

Take Pork and seeþ it wel and grinde it smale and medle it wiþ ayren & brede. ygrated. do þerto powdour fort and safroun with pyner & salt. take & close litull Balles in foiles [2] of sawge. wete it with a batour of ayren & fry it. & serue it forth.

    [1] Sawgeat. So named from the Sage, or *Sawge* [2] foiles. leaves.

CRYSPES [1]. XX.VIII. II.

Take flour of pandemayn and medle it with white grece ouer the fyrer in a chawfour [2] and do the batour þerto queyntlich [3] þurgh þy fyngours. or thurgh a skymour. and lat it a litul [4] quayle [5] a litell so þe þer be hool þerinne. And if þer wilt colour it wiþ alkenet yfoundyt. take hem up & cast þerinne sugur, and serue hem forth.

[1] Cryspes. Ms. Ed. No. 26. *Cryppys*, meaning *Crisps*, Chaucer having *crips*, by transposition, for *crisp*. In Kent *p* is commonly put before the *s*, as *haps* is *hasp*, *waps* is *wasp*. V. Junius. V. *Happs*, and *Haspe*, and *Wasp*. [2] chawfour. chaffing dish. [3] quentlich'. nicely. [4] a litul. Dele. [5] quayle. an cool?

CRYSPELS. XX.VIII. III.

Take and make a foile of gode Past as thynne as Paper. kerue it out & fry it in oile. oþer in þe [1] grece and þe remnaunt [2], take hony clarified and flaunne [3] þerwith, alye hem up and serue hem forth.

[1] þe grece. Dele *the*. [2] þe remnant, i. e. as for the remnant. [3] flaunne. French *flau*, custard.

TARTEE. XX.VIII. IIII.

Take pork ysode. hewe it & bray it. do þerto ayrenn. Raisouns sugur and powdour of gyngur. powdour douce. and smale briddes þeramong & white grece. take prunes, safroun. & salt, and make a crust in a trape & do þer Fars [1] þerin. & bake it wel & serue it forth.

[1] þer Fars, r. þe Fars.

TART IN YMBRE [1] DAY. XX.VIII. V.

Take and parboile Oynouns presse out þe water & hewe hem smale. take brede & bray it in a morter. and temper it up with Ayren. do þerto butter, safroun and salt. & raisouns corauns. & a litel sugur with powdour douce. and bake it in a trape. & serue it forth.

[1] Ymbre. Ember.

TART DE BRY [1]. XX.VIII. VI.

Take a Crust ynche depe in a trape. take zolkes of Ayren rawe & chese ruayn [2]. & medle it & þe zolkes togyder. and do þerto powdour gyngur. sugur. safroun. and salt. do it in a trape, bake it and serue it forth.

[1] de Bry. Qu. *Brie*, the country. [2] Chese ruayn. Qu. of Roisen. V. ad 49.

TART DE BRYMLENT [1]. XX.VIII. VII.

Take Fyges & Raysouns. & waisshe hem in Wyne. and grinde hem smale with apples & peres clene ypiked. take hem up and cast hem in a pot wiþ wyne and sugur. take salwar Salmoun [2] ysode. oþer codlyng, oþer haddok, & bray hem smal. & do þerto white powdours & hool spices. & salt. and seeþ it. and whanne it is sode ynowz. take it up and do it in a vessel and lat it kele. make a Coffyn an ynche depe & do þe fars þerin. Plaunt it boue [3] with prunes and damysyns. take þe stones out, and wiþ dates quarte rede [4] dand piked clene. and couere the coffyn, and bake it wel, and serue it forth.

[1] Brymlent. Perhaps Midlent or High Lent. *Bryme*, in Cotgrave, is the *midst* of Winter. The fare is certainly lenten. A.S. [Anglo-Saxon: bryme]. Solennis, or beginning of Lent, from A.S. [Anglo-Saxon:

brymm], ora, margo. Yet, after all, it may be a mistake for *Prymlent*.

[2] salwar Samoun. V. ad No. 98.

[3] plaunt it above. Stick it *above*, or on the top.

[4] quarte red. quartered.

TARTES OF FLESH [1]. XX.VIII. VIII.

Take Pork ysode and grynde it smale. tarde [2] harde eyrenn isode & ygrounde and do þerto with Chese ygronde. take gode powdour and hool spices, sugur, safroun, and salt & do þerto. make a coffyn as to feel sayde [3] & do þis þerinne, & plaunt it with smale briddes istyned & counyng. & hewe hem to smale gobettes & bake it as tofore. & serue it forth.

[1] Tartes of Flesh. So we have *Tarte Poleyn*, Lel. Coll. IV. p. 226. i.e. of Pullen, or Poultry. [2] tarde, r. *take*. For see No. 169. [3] to feel sayde. perhaps, *to hold the same*.

TARTLETES. XX.VIII. IX.

Take Veel ysode and grinde it smale. take harde Eyrenn isode and yground & do þerto with prunes hoole [1]. dates. icorue. pynes and Raisouns coraunce. hool spices & powdour. sugur. salt, and make a litell coffyn and do þis fars þerinne. & bake it & serue it forth.

[1] hoole, whole.

TARTES OF FYSSHE. XX.VIII. X.

Take Eelys and Samoun and smyte hem on pecys. & stewe it [1] in almaund mylke and verious. drawe up on almaund mylk wiþ þe stewe. Pyke out the bones clene of þe fyssh. and save þe myddell pece hoole of þe Eelys & grinde þat ooþer fissh smale. and do þerto powdour, sugur, & salt and grated brede. & fors þe Eelys þerwith þerer as [2] þe bonys were medle þe ooþer dele of the fars & þe mylk togider. and colour it with saundres. make a crust in a trape as before. and bake it þerin and serue it forth.

[1] it. rather hem, i.e. them. [2] þereras. where. V. No. 177.

SAMBOCADE [1]. XX.VIII. XI.

Take and make a Crust in a trape. & take a cruddes and wryng out þe wheyze. and drawe hem þurgh a straynour and put in þe straynour crustes. do þerto sugur the þridde part & somdel [2] whyte of Ayrenn. & shake þerin blomes of elren [3]. & bake it up with curose [4] & messe it forth.

[1] Sambucade. As made of the *Sambucus,* or Elder. [2] Somdel. Some. [3] Blom of Elren. Elder flowers. [4] curose.

ERBOLATES [1]. XX.VIII. XII.

Take parsel, myntes [2], sauerey, & sauge, tansey, veruayn, clarry, rewe, ditayn, fenel, southrenwode, hewe hem & grinde hem smale, medle hem up with Ayrenn. do butter in a trape. & do þe fars þerto. & bake it & messe it forth.

[1] Erbolat, i.e. Herbolade, a confection of herbs. [2] myntes, mint.

NYSEBEK [1]. XX.VIII. XIII.

Take þere þridde part of sowre Dokkes and flour þerto. & bete it togeder tyl it be as towh as eny lyme. cast þerto salt. & do it in a disshe holke [2] in þe bothom, and let it out wiþ þy finger queynchche [3] in a chowfer [4] wiþ oile. & frye it wel. and whan it is ynowhz: take it out and cast þerto suger &c.

[1] Nysebek. Qu. [2] holke. Qu. hollow. [3] queynchche. an *queyntlich'*, as No. 162. [4] Chowfer. chaffing dish, as No. 162.

FOR TO MAKE POMME DORRYLE [1] AND OÞER ÞNGES. XX.VIII. XIIII.

Take þe lire of Pork rawe. and grynde it smale. medle it up wiþ powdre fort, safroun, and salt, and do þerto Raisouns of Coraunce, make balles þerof. and wete it wele in white of ayrenn. & do it to seeþ in boillyng water. take hem up and put hem on a spyt. rost hem wel and take parsel ygronde and wryng it up with ayren & a party of flour. and lat erne [2] aboute þe spyt. And if þou wilt, take for parsel safroun, and serue it forth.

[1] Pomme dorryle. Contents, *pom dorryes*, rectè, for MS. Ed. 42, has *Pommedorry*; and see No. 177. So named from the *balls* and *the gilding*. "Pommes dorées, golden apples." Cotgrave. *Poundorroye*. MS. Ed. 58; but vide *Dorry* in Gloss.

[2] erne. Qu.

COTAGRES [1]. XX.VIII. XV.

Take and make þe self fars [2]. but do þerto pynes and sugur. take an hole rowsted cok, pulle hym [3] & hylde [4] hym al togyder saue þe legges. take a pigg and hilde [5] hym fro þe myddes dounward, fylle him ful of þe fars

& sowe hym fast togider. do hym in a panne & seeþ hym wel. and whan þei bene isode: do hem on a spyt & rost it wele. colour it with zolkes of ayren and safroun, lay þeron foyles [6] of gold and of siluer. and serue hit forth.

[1] Cotagres. This is a sumptuous dish. Perhaps we should read *Cokagres*, from the *cock* and *grees*, or wild pig, therein used. V. *vyne grace* in Gloss. [2] self fars. Same as preceding Recipe. [3] pulle hym, i.e. in pieces. [4] hylde. cast. [5] hilde. skin. [6] foyles. leaves; of Laurel or Bay, suppose; gilt and silvered for ornament.

HERT ROWEE [1]. XX.VIII. XVI.

Take þer mawe of þe grete Swyne. and fyfe oþer sex of pigges mawe. fyll hem full of þe self fars. & sowe hem fast, perboile hem. take hem up & make smale prews [2] of gode past and frye hem. take þese prews yfryed & seeþ [3] hem þicke in þe mawes on þe fars made after [4] an urchoun withoute legges. put hem on a spyt & roost hem & colour hem with safroun & messe hem forth.

[1] Hert rowee. Contents, *Hart rows*; perhaps from *heart*. [2] prews. Qu. V. in Gloss. [3] seeþ. There is a fault here; it means stick. [4] after, i. e. like.

POTEWS [1]. XX.VIII. XVII.

Take Pottes of Erþe lytell of half a quart and fyll hem full of fars of pomme dorryes [2]. oþer make with þyn honde. oþer in a moolde pottes of þe self fars. put hem in water & seeþ hem up wel. and whan þey buth ynowz. breke þe pottes of erþe & do þe fars on þe spyt & rost hem wel. and whan þei buth yrosted. colour hem as pomme dorryes. make of litull prewes [3] gode past, frye hem oþer rost hem wel in grece. & make þerof Eerys [4] to pottes & colour it. and make rosys [5] of gode past, & frye hem, & put þe steles [6] in þe hole þer [7] þe spyt was. & colour it with whyte. oþer rede. & serue it forth.

[1] Potews. probably from the *pots* employed. [2] pomme dorryes. Vide ad No. 174. [3] prewes. V. ad 176. [4] eerys. Ears *for* the pots. V. 185. [5] rosys. roses. [6] sleles. stalks. [7] þer. there, i.e. where. V. 170.

SACHUS [1]. XX.VIII. XVIII.

Take smale Sachellis of canuas and fille hem full of þe same fars [2] & seeþ hem. and whan þey buth ynowz take of the canvas, rost hem & colour hem &c.

[1] Sachus. I suppose *sacks*. [2] same fars. viz. as 174.

BURSEWS [1]. XX.VIII. XIX.

Take Pork, seeþ it and grynde it smale wiþ sodden ayren. do þerto gode powdours and hole spices and salt with sugur. make þerof smale balles, and cast hem in a batour [2] of ayren. & wete hem in flour. and frye hem in grece as frytours [3]. and serue hem forth.

[1] Bursews. Different from *Bursen* in No. 11; therefore qu. etymon. [2] Batour. batter. [3] frytours. fritters.

SPYNOCHES [1] YFRYED. XX.IX.

Take Spynoches. perboile hem in seþyng water. take hem up and presse . . . out of þe water [2] and hem [3] in two. frye hem in oile clene. & do þerro powdour. & serue forth.

[1] Spynoches. Spinage, which we use in the singular. [2] out of the water. dele *of*; or it may mean, *when out of the water*. [3] hem r. *hewe*.

BENES YFRYED. XX.IX. I.

Take benes and seeþ hem almost til þey bersten. take and wryng out þer water clene. do þerto Oynouns ysode and ymynced. and garlec þerwith. frye hem in oile. oþer in grece. & do þerto powdour douce. & serue it forth.

RYSSHEWS [1] OF FRUYT. XX.IX. II.

Take Fyges and raisouns. pyke hem and waisshe hem in Wyne. grynde hem wiþ apples and peeres. ypared and ypiked clene. do þerto gode powdours. and hole spices. make bailes þerof. fryen in oile and serue hem forth.

[1] Rysshews. *russhewses*, Contents. Qu.

DARYOLS [1]. XX.IX. III.

Take Creme of Cowe mylke. oþer of Almandes. do þerto ayren with sugur, safroun, and salt, medle it yfere. do it in a coffyn. of II. ynche depe. bake it wel and serue it forth,

[1] Daryols. Qu.

FLAUMPENS [1]. XX.IX. IIII.

Take fat Pork ysode. pyke it clene. grynde it smale. grynde Chese & do þerto. wiþ sugur and gode powdours. make a coffyn of an ynche depe. and do þis fars þerin. make a thynne foile of gode past & kerue out þeroff smale poyntes [2]. frye hem in fars [3]. & bake it up &c.

[1] Flaumpeyns. *Flaumpens*, Contents. V. No. 113. [2] Points, seems the same as *Prews*, No. 176. [3] in fars, f. *in the fars*; and yet the Fars is disposed of before; ergo quære.

CHEWETES [1] ON FLESSHE DAY. XX.IX. V.

Take þer lire of Pork and kerue it al to pecys. and hennes þerwith and do it in a panne and frye it & make a Coffyn as to [2] a pye smale & do þerinne. & do þeruppon zolkes of ayrenn. harde. powdour of gyngur and salt, couere it & fry it in grece. oþer bake it wel and serue it forth.

[1] Chewets. V. 186. [2] as to, as for. V. No. 177.

CHEWETES ON FYSSH DAY. XX.IX. VI.

Take Turbut. haddok. Codlyng. and hake. and seeþ it. grynde it smale. and do þerto Dates. ygrounden. raysouns pynes. gode powdoer and salt. make a Coffyn as tofore saide. close þis þerin. and frye it in oile. oþer stue it in gyngur. sugur. oþer in wyne. oþer bake it. & serue forth.

HASTLETES [1] OF FRUYT. XX.IX. VII.

Take Fyges iquarterid [2]. Raysouns hool dates and Almandes hoole. and ryne [3] hem on a spyt and roost hem. and endore [4] hem as pomme dorryes & serue hem forth.

[1] Hastletes. *Hasteletes*, Contents. [2] iquarterid. iquartered. [3] ryne. run. [4] endore. endorse, MS. Ed. 42. II. 6. v. ad 147.

COMADORE [1]. XX.IX. VII.

Take Fyges and Raisouns. pyke hem and waisshe hem clene, skalde hem in wyne. grynde hem right smale, cast sugur in þe self wyne. and founde it togyder. drawe it up thurgh a straynour. & alye up þe fruyt þerwith. take gode peerys and Apples. pare hem and take þe best, grynde hem smale and cast þerto. set a pot on þe fuyrer [2] wiþ oyle and cast alle þise þynges þerinne. and stere it warliche, and kepe it wel fro brennyng. and whan it is fyned cast þerto powdours of gynger of canel. of galyngale. hool clowes flour of canel. & macys hoole. cast þerto pynes a litel fryed in oile & salt, and whan it is ynowz fyned: take it up and do it in a vessel & lat it kele. and whan it is colde: kerue out with a knyf smale pecys of þe gretnesse & of þe length of a litel fyngur. & close it fast in gode past. & frye hen in oile. & serue forth.

[1] Comadore. Qu. [2] Fuyr. fire.

CHASTLETES [1], XX.IX. IX.

Take and make a foyle of gode past with a roller of a foot brode. & lyngur[2] by cumpas. make iiii Coffyns of þe self past uppon þe rolleres þe gretnesse of þe smale of þyn Arme. of vi ynche depnesse. make þe gretust [3] in þe myddell. fasten þe foile in þe mouth upwarde. & fasten þee [4] oþere foure in euery syde. kerue out keyntlich kyrnels [5] above in þe manere of bataiwyng [6] and drye hem harde in an Ovene. oþer in þe Sunne. In þe myddel Coffyn do a fars of Pork with gode Pork & ayrenn rawe wiþ salt. & colour it wiþ safroun and do in anoþer Creme of Almandes. and helde [7] it in anoþer [8] creme of Cowe mylke with ayrenn. colour it with saundres.

anoþur manur. Fars of Fygur. of raysouns. of Apples. of Peeres. & holde it in broun [9].

anoþer manere. do fars as to frytours blanched. and colour it with grene. put þis to þe ovene & bake it wel. & serue it forth with ew ardaunt [10].

[1] Chastelets. Litlle castles, as is evident from the kernelling and the battlements mentioned. *Castles of jelly templewise made.* Lel. Coll. IV. p. 227. [2] lynger. longer. [3] gretust. greatest. [4] þee, i. e. thou. [5] kyrnels. Battlements. V. Gloss. Keyntlich, quaintly, curiously. V. Gloss. [6] bataiwyng. embatteling. [7] helde. put, cast. [8] another. As the middle one and only two more are provided for, the two remaining were to be filled, I presume, in the same manner alternately. [9] holde it broun. make it brown. [10] ew ardaunt. hot water. *Eau*, water; anciently written *eue*.

FOR TO MAKE II. [1] PECYS OF FLESSH TO FASTEN TOGYDER. XX.IX. X.

Take a pece of fressh Flesh and do it in a pot for to seeþ. or take a pece of fressh Flessh and kerue it al to gobetes. do it in a pot to seeþ. & take þe wose [2] of comfery & put it in þe pot to þe flessh & it shal fasten anon, & so serue it forth.

[1] II. *Twey*, Contents.
[2] wose. Roots of comfrey are of a very glutinous nature. Quincy.
　　Dispens. p. 100. *Wose* is A.S. [Anglo-Saxon: paer], *humour*,
　　juice. See Junius. v. *Wos*, and Mr. Strype's Life of Stow, p. VIII.

PUR FAIT YPOCRAS [1]. XX.IX. XI. Treys Unces de canett. & iii unces de gyngeuer. spykenard de Spayn le pays dun denerer [2], garyngale [3]. clowes, gylofre. poeurer long [4], noiez mugadez [5]. maziozame [6] cardemonij [7] de chescun i. quart' douce [8] grayne & [9] de paradys stour de queynel [10] de chescun dim [11] unce de toutes, soit fait powdour &c.

[1] Pur fait Ypocras. Id est, *Pour faire Ypocras*; a whole pipe of which was provided for archbishop Nevill's feast about A.D. 1466, So that it was in vast request formerly. [2] le pays d'un denerer, i.e. *le pays d'un Denier*. [3] garyngale, i.e. *galyngale*. [4] poeurer long, r. poiurer long, i.e. *poivre long*. [5] mugadez, r. muscadez; but q. as the French is *muguette*. Nutmegs. [6] maziozame, r. *marjorame*. [7] Cardemonij, r. *Cardamones*. [8] quartdouce, r. *d'once*.. Five penny weights. [9] &. dele. [10] queynel. Perhaps *Canell*; but qu. as that is named before. [11] dim. dimid.

FOR TO MAKE BLANK MAUNGER [1]. XX.IX. XII.

Put Rys in water al a nyzt and at morowe waisshe hem clene, afterward put hem to þe fyre fort [2] þey berst & not to myche. ssithen [3] take brawn of Capouns, or of hennes. soden & drawe [4] it smale. after take mylke of Almandes. and put in to þe Ryys & boile it. and whan it is yboiled put in þe brawn & alye it þerwith. þat it be wel chargeaunt [5] and mung it fynelich' [6] wel þat it sit not [7] to þe pot. and whan it is ynowz & chargeaunt. do þerto sugur gode part, put þerin almandes. fryed in white grece. & dresse it forth.

[1] blank maunger. Very different from that we make now. V. 36. [2] fyre fort. strong fire. [3] ssithen. then. [4] drawe. make. [5] chargeaunt. stiff. So below, *ynowhz & chargeaunt*. V.193, 194. V. Gloss. [6] mung it fynelich' wel. stir it very well. [7] sit not. adheres not, and thereby burns not. Used now in the North.

FOR TO MAKE BLANK DESNE [1]. XX.IX. XIII.

Take Brawn of Hennes or of Capouns ysoden withoute þe skyn. & hewe hem as smale as þou may. & grinde hem in a morter. after take gode mylke of Almandes & put þe brawn þerin. & stere it wel togyder & do hem to seeþ. & take flour of Rys & amydoun & alay it. so þat it be chargeant. & do þerto sugur a gode party. & a party of white grece. and when it is put in disshes strewe uppon it blaunche powdour, and þenne put in blank desire and mawmenye [2] in disshes togider. And serue forth.

[1] blank *Desne. Desire,* Contents; rectè. V. Gloss. The Recipe in MS. Ed. 29 is much the same with this. [2] Mawmenye. See No. 194.

FOR TO MAKE MAWMENNY [1]. XX.IX. XIIII. Take þe chese and of Flessh of Capouns or of Hennes. & hakke smale in a morter. take mylke of Almandes with þe broth of freissh Beef, oþer freissh flessh. & put the flessh in þe mylke oþer in the broth and set hem to þe frye [2]. & alye hem up with flour of Ryse. or gastbon [3]. or amydoun. as chargeant as with blanke desire. & with zolkes of ayren and safroun for to make it zelow. and when it is dressit in disshes with blank desire styk above clowes de gilofre. & strewe Powdour of galyngale above. and serue it forth.

[1] Mawmenny. *Mawmoune,* Contents. *Maumene* MS. Ed. 29. 30. vide No. 193. See Preface for a *fac-simile* of this Recipe. [2] þe frye. an fyre? [3] gastbon. Qu.

THE PETY PERUAUNT [1]. XX.IX. XV. Take male Marow [2]. hole parade [3] and kerue it rawe. powdour of Gynger. zolkes of Ayrenn, dates mynced. raisouns of coraunce. salt a lytel. & loke þat þou make þy past with zolkes of Ayren. & þat no water come þerto. and forme þy coffyn. and make up þy past.

[1] pety peruaunt. a paste; therefore, perhaps, *paty*; but qu. the latter word. [2] male Marow. Qu. [3] parade. Qu.

PAYN PUFF [1]. XX.IX. XVI. Eodem modo fait payn puff. but make it more tendre þe past. and loke þe past be rounde of þe payn puf as a coffyn & a pye.

[1] Payn puff. Contents has, *And the pete puant.*

[1]XPLICIT.

[1] A blank was left in the original for a large *E*.

THE FOLLOWING MEMORANDUM AT THE END OF THE ROLL.

"Antiquum hoc monumentum oblatum et missum est majestati vestræ vicesimo septimo die mensis Julij, anno regno vestri fælicissimi vicesimo viij ab humilimo vestro subdito, vestræque, majestati fidelissimo

EDWARD STAFFORD, Hæres domus subversæ Buckinghamiens."

N.B. He was Lord Stafford and called Edward.

Edw. D. of Bucks beheaded 1521. 13 H. VIII.
|
Henry, restored in blood by H. VIII.; and again 1 Ed. VI.
|
Edw. aged 21, 1592; born 1592. 21. ob. 1525. f. 1625.
| 21
Edw. b. 1600. ———
       1571 born.

ANCIENT COOKERY. A.D. 1381.

Hic incipiunt universa servicia tam de carnibus quam de pissibus [1].

I. FOR TO MAKE FURMENTY [1].

Nym clene Wete and bray it in a morter wel that the holys [2] gon al of and seyt [3] yt til it breste and nym yt up. and lat it kele [4] and nym fayre fresch broth and swete mylk of Almandys or swete mylk of kyne and temper yt al. and nym the yolkys of eyryn [5]. boyle it a lityl and set yt adoun and messe yt forthe wyth fat venyson and fresh moton.

[1] See again, No. I. of the second part of this treatise. [2] Hulls. [3] Miswritten for *seyth* or *sethe*, i.e. seeth. [4] cool. [5] eggs.

II. FOR TO MAKE PISE of ALMAYNE.

Nym wyte Pisyn and wasch hem and seth hem a good wyle sithsyn wasch hem in golde [1] watyr unto the holys gon of alle in a pot and kever it wel that no breth passe owt and boyle hem ryzt wel and do therto god mylk of Almandys and a party of flowr of ris and salt and safron and messe yt forthe.

[1] cold.

III.

Cranys and Herons schulle be euarund [1] wyth Lardons of swyne and rostyd and etyn wyth gyngynyr.

[1] Perhaps *enarmed,* or *enorned.* See Mr. Brander's Roll, No. 146.

IV.

Pecokys and Partrigchis schul ben yparboyld and lardyd and etyn wyth gyngenyr.

V. MORTERELYS [1].

Nym hennyn and porke and seth hem togedere nym the lyre [2] of the hennyn and the porke and hakkyth finale and grynd hit al to dust and wyte bred therwyth and temper it wyth the selve broth and wyth heyryn and colure it with safroun and boyle it and disch it and cast theron powder of peper and of gyngynyr and serve it forthe.

[1] V. Mortrews in Gloss. [2] Flesh.

VI. CAPONYS INC ONEYS.

Schal be sodyn. Nym the lyre and brek it smal In a morter and peper and wyte bred therwyth and temper it wyth ale and ley it wyth the capoun. Nym hard sodyn eyryn and hewe the wyte smal and kaste thereto and nym the zolkys al hole and do hem in a dysch and boyle the capoun and colowre it wyth safroun and salt it and messe it forthe.

VII. HENNYS [1] IN BRUET.

Schullyn be scaldyd and sodyn wyth porke and grynd pepyr and comyn bred and ale and temper it wyth the selve broth and boyle and colowre it wyth safroun and salt it and messe it forthe.

[1] Hens.

VIII. HARYS [1] IN CMEE [2].

Schul be parboylyd and lardyd and rostid and nym onyons and myce hem rizt smal and fry hem in wyte gres and grynd peper bred and ale and the onions therto and coloure it wyth safroun and salt it and serve it forth.

[1] Hares. [1] Perhaps *Cinee*; for see No. 51.

IX. HARIS IN TALBOTAYS.

Schul be hewe in gobbettys and sodyn with al the blod Nym bred piper and ale and grynd togedere and temper it with the selve broth and boyle it and salt it and serve it forthe.

X. CONYNGGYS [1] IN GRAVEY.

Schul be sodyn and hakkyd in gobbettys and grynd gyngynyr galyngale and canel. and temper it up with god almand mylk and boyle it and nym macys and clowys and kest [2] therin and the conynggis also and salt hym [3] and serve it forthe.

[1] Rabbits. [2] Cast. [3] *it*, or perhaps *hem*.

XI. FOR TO MAKE A COLYS [1].

Nym hennys and schald hem wel. and seth hem after and nym the lyre and hak yt smal and bray it with otyn grotys in a morter and with wyte bred and temper it up wyth the broth Nym the grete bonys and grynd hem al to dust and kest hem al in the broth and mak it thorw a clothe and boyle it and serve it forthe.

[1] Cullis. V. Preface.

XII. FOR TO MAKE NOMBLES [1].

Nym the nomblys of the venysoun and wasch hem clene in water and salt hem and seth hem in tweye waterys grynd pepyr bred and ale and temper it wyth the secunde brothe and boyle it and hak the nomblys and do theryn and serve it forthe.

[1] Umbles.

XIII. FOR TO MAKE BLANCHE BREWET DE ALYNGYN.

Nym kedys [1] and chekenys and hew hem in morsellys and seth hem in almand mylk or in kyne mylke grynd gyngyner galingale and cast therto and boyle it and serve it forthe.

[1] Kids.

XIV. FOR TO MAKE BLOMANGER [1].

Nym rys and lese hem and wasch hem clene and do thereto god almande mylk and seth hem tyl they al to brest and than lat hem kele and nym the lyre of the hennyn or of capouns and grynd hem smal kest therto wite grese and boyle it Nym blanchyd almandys and safroun and set hem above in the dysche and serve yt forthe.

[1] Blanc-manger. See again, No. 33, 34. II. No. 7. Chaucer writes it *Blankmanger*.

XV. FOR TO MAKE AFRONCHEMOYLE [1].

Nym eyren wyth al the wyte and myse bred and schepys [2] talwe as gret as dyses [3] grynd peper and safroun and cast therto and do hit in the schepis wombe seth it wel and dresse it forthe of brode leches thynne.

[1] Frenchemulle d'un mouton. A sheeps call, or kell. Cotgrave. Junius, v. *Moil*, says, "a French moile Chaucero est cibus delicatior, a dish made of marrow and grated bread." [2] Sheep's fat. [3] dice; square bits, or bits as big as dice.

XVI. FOR TO MAKE BRYMEUS.

Nym the tharmys [1] of a pygge and wasch hem clene in water and salt and seth hem wel and than hak hem smale and grynd pepyr and safroun bred and ale and boyle togedere Nym wytys of eyrynn and knede it wyth flour and mak smal pelotys [2] and fry hem with wyte grees and do hem in disches above that othere mete and serve it forthe.

[1] Rops, guts, puddings [2] Balls, pellets, from the French *pelote*.

XVII. FOR TO MAKE APPULMOS [1].

Nym appelyn and seth hem and lat hem kele and make hem thorw a clothe and on flesch dayes kast therto god fat breyt [2] of Bef and god wyte grees and sugar and safroun and almande mylk on fysch dayes oyle de olyve and gode powdres [3] and serve it forthe.

[1] See No. 35. [2] Breth, i. e. broth. See No. 58. [3] Spices ground small. See No. 27, 28. 35. 58. II. No. 4. 17. or perhaps of Galingale. II. 20. 24.

XVIII. FOR TO MAKE A FROYS [1].

Nym Veel and seth it wel and hak it smal and grynd bred peper and safroun and do thereto and frye yt and presse it wel upon a bord and dresse yt forthe.

[1] a Fraise

XIX. FOR TO MAKE FRUTURS [1].

Nym flowre and eyryn and grynd peper and safroun and mak therto a batour and par aplyn and kyt hem to brode penys [2] and kest hem theryn and fry hem in the batour wyth fresch grees and serve it forthe.

[1] Fritters. [2] Pieces as broad as pennies, or perhaps pecys.

XX. FOR TO MAKE CHANKE [1].

Nym Porke and seth it wel and hak yt smal nym eyryn wyth al the wytys and swyng hem wel al togedere and kast god swete mylke thereto and boyle yt and messe it forthe.

[1] Quære.

XXI. FOR TO MAKE JUSSEL.

Nym eyryn wyth al the wytys and mice bred grynd pepyr and safroun and do therto and temper yt wyth god fresch broth of porke and boyle it wel and messe yt forthe.

XXII. FOR TO MAKE GEES [1] IN OCHEPOT [2].

Nym and schald hem wel and hew hem wel in gobettys al rawe and seth hem in her owyn grees and cast therto wyn or ale a cuppe ful and myce onyons smal and do therto and boyle yt and salt yt and messe yt forthe.

[1] Gese. [2] Hochepot. Vide Gloss.

XXIII. FOR TO MAKE EYRYN IN BRUET.

Nym water and welle [1] yt and brek eyryn and kast theryn and grynd peper and safroun and temper up wyth swete mylk and boyle it and hakke chese smal and cast theryn and messe yt forthe.

[1] Quære the meaning.

XXIV. FOR TO MAKE CRAYTOUN [1].

Tak checonys and schald hem and seth hem and grvnd gyngen' other pepyr and comyn and temper it up wyth god mylk and do the checonys theryn and boyle hem and serve yt forthe.

[1] Vide ad No. 60 of the Roll.

XXV. FOR TO MAKE MYLK ROST.

Nym swete mylk and do yt in a panne nyn [1] eyryn wyth al the wyte and swyng hem wel and cast therto and colowre yt wyth safroun and boyl it tyl yt wexe thikke and thanne seth [2] yt thorw a culdore [3] and nym that, leyyth [4] and presse yt up on a bord and wan yt ys cold larde it and scher yt on schyverys and roste yt on a grydern and serve yt forthe.

[1] Read *nym*. [2] strain. See No. 27. [3] Cuilinder. [4] That which is left in the cullinder.

XXVI. FOR TO MAKE CRYPPYS [1].

Nym flour and wytys of eyryn sugur other hony and sweyng togedere and mak a batour nym wyte grees and do yt in a posnet and cast the batur thereyn and stury to thou have many [2] and tak hem up and messe hem wyth the frutours and serve forthe.

[1] Meaning, *crisps*. V. Gloss. [2] It will run into lumps, I suppose.

XXVII. FOR TO MAKE BERANDYLES [1].

Nym Hennys and seth hem wyth god Buf and wan hi ben sodyn nym the Hennyn and do awey the bonys and bray smal yn a mortar and temper yt wyth the broth and seth yt thorw a culdore and cast therto powder of gyngenyr and sugur and graynys of powmis gernatys [2] and boyle yt and dresse yt in dysches and cast above clowys gylofres [3] and maces and god powder [4] serve yt forthe.

[1] Quære the meaning. [2] Pomegranates. V. No. 39. [3] Not clove-gilliflowers, but *cloves*. See No. 30, 31, 40. [4] See No. 17, note [3].

XXVIII. FOR TO MAKE CAPONS IN CASSELYS.

Nym caponys and schald hem nym a penne and opyn the skyn at the hevyd [1] and blowe hem tyl the skyn ryse from the flesshe and do of the skyn al hole and seth the lyre of Hennyn and zolkys of heyryn and god powder and make a Farsure [2] and fil ful the skyn and parboyle yt and do yt on a spete and rost yt and droppe [3] yt wyth zolkys of eyryn and god powder rostyng and nym the caponys body and larde yt and roste it and nym almaunde mylk and amydoun [4] and mak a batur and droppe the body rostyng and serve yt forthe.

[1] Head. Sax. [Anglo-Saxon: heofod] and [Anglo-Saxon: hevod], hence our *Head*. [2] stuffing. [3] baste. [4] Vide Gloss.

XXIX. FOR TO MAKE THE BLANK SURRY [1].

Tak brann [2] of caponys other of hennys and the thyes [3] wythowte the skyn and kerf hem smal als thou mayst and grynd hem smal in a morter and tak mylk of Almaundys and do yn the branne and grynd hem thanne togedere and and seth hem togeder' and tak flour of rys other amydoun and lye it that yt be charchant and do therto sugur a god parti and a party of wyt grees and boyle yt and wan yt ys don in dyschis straw upon blank poudere and do togedere blank de sury and manmene [4] in a dysch and serve it forthe.

[1] Vide *Blank Desire* in Gloss. [2] Perhaps *brawn*, the brawny part. See No. 33, and the Gloss. [3] Thighs. [4] See the next number. Quære *Mawmeny*.

XXX. FOR TO MAKE MANMENE [1].

Tak the thyys [2] other the flesch of the caponys fede [3] hem and kerf hem smal into a morter and tak mylk of Almandys wyth broth of fresch Buf and do the flesch in the mylk or in the broth and do yt to the fyre and myng yt togedere wyth flour of Rys othere of wastelys als charchaut als the blank de sure and wyth the zolkys of eyryn for to make it zelow and safroun and wan yt ys dressyd in dysches wyth blank de sure straw upon clowys of gelofre [4] and straw upon powdre of galentyn and serve yt forthe.

 [1] Vide Number 29, and the Gloss. [2] Thighs. [3] Quære. [4] See No. 27, note [3].

XXXI. FOR TO MAKE BRUET OF ALMAYNE.

Tak Partrichys rostyd and checonys and qualys rostyd and larkys ywol and demembre the other and mak a god cawdel and dresse the flesch in a dysch and strawe powder of galentyn therupon. styk upon clowys of gelofre and serve yt forthe.

XXXII. FOR RO MAKE BRUET OF LOMBARDYE.

Tak chekenys or hennys or othere flesch and mak the colowre als red as any blod and tak peper and kanel and gyngyner bred [1] and grynd hem in a morter and a porcion of bred and mak that bruer thenne and do that flesch in that broth and mak hem boyle togedere and stury it wel and tak eggys and temper hem wyth Jus of Parcyle and wryng hem thorwe a cloth and wan that bruet is boylyd do that therto and meng tham togedere wyth fayr grees so that yt be fat ynow and serve yt forthe.

 [1] This is still in use, and, it seems, is an old compound.

XXXIII. FOR TO MAKE BLOMANGER [1].

Do Ris in water al nyzt and upon the morwe wasch hem wel and do hem upon the fyre for to [2] they breke and nozt for to muche and tak Brann [3] of Caponis sodyn and wel ydraw [4] and smal and tak almaund mylk and boyle it wel wyth ris and wan it is yboylyd do the flesch therin so that it be charghaunt and do therto a god party of sugure and wan it ys dressyd forth in dischis straw theron blaunche Pouder and strik [5] theron Almaundys fryed wyt wyte grece [6] and serve yt forthe.

[1] See No. 14. [2] till. *for*, however, abounds. [3] See No. 29. note d. [4] Perhaps, *strained*. See No. 49; and Part II. No. 33. [5] Perhaps, *stik*, i.e. stick; but see 34. [6] Grese. Fat, or lard.

XXXIV. FOR TO MAKE SANDALE THAT PARTY TO BLOMANGER.

Tak Flesch of Caponys and of Pork sodyn kerf yt smal into a morter togedere and bray that wel. and temper it up wyth broth of Caponys and of Pork that yt be wel charchaunt also the crem of Almaundys and grynd egges and safroun or sandres togedere that it be coloured and straw upon Powder of Galentyn and strik thereon clowys and maces and serve it forthe.

XXXV. FOR TO MAKE APULMOS [1].

Tak Applys and seth hem and let hem kele and after mak hem thorwe a cloth and do hem im a pot and kast to that mylk of Almaundys wyth god broth of Buf in Flesch dayes do bred ymyed [2] therto. And the fisch dayes do therto oyle of olyve and do therto sugur and colour it wyth safroun and strew theron Powder and serve it forthe.

[1] See No. 8.

LII. FOR TO MAKE A BUKKENADE [1].

Tak veel and boyle it tak zolkys of eggys and mak hem thykke tak macis and powdre of gyngyner and powder of peper and boyle yt togeder and messe yt forth.

[1] Vide No. 45.

LIII. FOR TO MAKE A ROO BROTH [1].

Tak Parsile and Ysop and Sauge and hak yt smal boil it in wyn and in

water and a lytyl powdre of peper and messe yt forth.

[1] *Deer* or *Roes* are not mentioned, as in Mr. Brander's Roll, No. 14, ergo quære. It is a meager business. Can it mean *Rue-Broth* for penitents?

LIV. FOR TO MAK A BRUET OF SARCYNESSE.

Tak the lyre of the fresch Buf and bet it al in pecis and bred and fry yt in fresch gres tak it up and and drye it and do yt in a vessel wyth wyn and sugur and powdre of clowys boyle yt togedere tyl the flesch have drong the liycoure and take the almande mylk and quibibz macis and clowys and boyle hem togedere tak the flesch and do thereto and messe it forth.

LV. FOR TO MAKE A GELY [1].

Tak hoggys fet other pyggys other erys other partrichys other chiconys and do hem togedere and serh [2] hem in a pot and do hem in flowre of canel and clowys other or grounde [3] do thereto vineger and tak and do the broth in a clene vessel of al thys and tak the Flesch and kerf yt in smal morselys and do yt therein tak powder of galyngale and cast above and lat yt kels tak bronches of the lorer tre and styk over it and kep yt al so longe as thou wilt and serve yt forth.

[1] Jelly. [2] seþ, i. e. *seeth*. [3] Not clearly expressed. It means either Cinamon or Cloves, and either in flour or ground.

LVI. FOR TO KEPE VENISON FRO RESTYNG.

Tak venisoun wan yt ys newe and cuver it hastely wyth Fern that no wynd may come thereto and wan thou hast ycuver yt wel led yt hom and do yt in a soler that sonne ne wynd may come thereto and dimembre it and do yt in a clene water and lef yt ther' half a day and after do yt up on herdeles for to drie and wan yt ys drye tak salt and do after thy venisoun axit [1] and do yt boyle in water that yt be other [2] so salt als water of the see and moche more and after lat the water be cold that it be thynne and thanne do thy Venisoun in the water and lat yt be therein thre daies and thre nyzt [3] and after tak yt owt of the water and salt it wyth drie salt ryzt wel in a barel and wan thy barel ys ful cuver it hastely that sunne ne wynd come thereto.

[1] as thy venison requires. See Gloss. to Chaucer for *axe*. [2] Dele. [3] A plural, as in No. 57.

LVII. FOR TO DO AWAY RESTYN [1] OF VENISOUN.

Tak the Venisoun that ys rest and do yt in cold water and after mak an hole in the herthe and lat yt be thereyn thre dayes and thre nyzt and after tak yt up and spot yt wel wyth gret salt of peite [2] there were the restyng ys and after lat yt hange in reyn water al nyzt or more.

[1] Restiness. It should be rather *restyng*. See below. [2] Pierre, or Petre.

LVIII. FOR TO MAKE POUNDORROGE [1].

Tak Partrichis wit [2] longe filettis of Pork al raw and hak hem wel smale and bray hem in a morter and wan they be wel brayed do thereto god plente of pouder and zolkys of eyryn and after mak thereof a Farsure formed of the gretnesse of a onyoun and after do it boyle in god breth of Buf other of Pork after lat yt kele and after do it on a broche of Hasel and do them to the fere to roste and after mak god bature of floure and egge on bature wyt and another zelow and do thereto god plente of sugur and tak a fethere or a styk and tak of the bature and peynte thereon above the applyn so that on be wyt and that other zelow wel colourd.

[1] Vide No. 42. [2] with.

EXPLICIT SERVICIUM DE CARNIBUS.

Hic incipit Servicium de Pissibus_ [1].

[1] See p. 1

I. FOR TO MAKE EGARDUSE [1].

Tak Lucys [2] or Tenchis and hak hem smal in gobette and fry hem in oyle de olive and syth nym vineger and the thredde party of sugur and myncyd onyons smal and boyle al togedere and cast thereyn clowys macys and quibibz and serve yt forthe.

[1] See No. 21 below, and part I. No. 50. [2] Lucy, I presume, means the *Pike*; so that this fish was known here long before the reign of H. VIII. though it is commonly thought otherwise. V. Gloss.

II. FOR TO MAKE RAPY [1].

Tak pyg' or Tenchis or other maner fresch fysch and fry yt wyth oyle de olive and syth nym the crustys of wyt bred and canel and bray yt al wel in a mortere and temper yt up wyth god wyn and cole [2] yt thorw an hersyve and that yt be al cole [3] of canel and boyle yt and cast therein hole clowys and macys and quibibz and do the fysch in dischis and rape [4] abovyn and dresse yt forthe.

[1] Vide No. 49. [2] Strain, from Lat. *colo*. [3] Strained, or cleared. [4] This Rape is what the dish takes its name from. Perhaps means *grape* from the French *raper*. Vide No. 28.

III. FOR TO MAKE FYGEY.

Nym Lucys or tenchis and hak hem in morsell' and fry hem tak vyneger and the thredde party of sugur myncy onyons smal and boyle al togedyr cast ther'yn macis clowys quibibz and serve yt forth.

IIII. FOR TO MAKE POMMYS MORLES.

Nym Rys and bray hem [1] wel and temper hem up wyth almaunde mylk and boyle yt nym applyn and par' hem and sher hem smal als dicis and cast hem ther'yn after the boylyng and cast sugur wyth al and colowr yt wyth safroun and cast ther'to pouder and serve yt forthe.

[1] Rice, as it consists of grains, is here considered as a plural. See also No. 5. 7, 8.

V. FOR TO MAKE RYS MOYLE [1].

Nym rys and bray hem ryzt wel in a morter and cast ther'to god Almaunde mylk and sugur and salt boyle yt and serve yt forth.

[1] Vide Gloss.

VI. FOR TO MAKE SOWPYS DORRY.

Nym onyons and mynce hem smale and fry hem in oyl dolyf Nym wyn and boyle yt wyth the onyouns roste wyte bred and do yt in dischis and god Almande mylk also and do ther'above and serve yt forthe.

VII. FOR TO MAKE BLOMANGER [1] OF FYSCH.

Tak a pound of rys les hem wel and wasch and seth tyl they breste and lat hem kele and do ther'to mylk of to pound of Almandys nym the

Perche or the Lopuster and boyle yt and kest sugur and salt also ther'to and serve yt forth.

[1] See note on No. 14. of Part I.

VIII. FOR TO MAKE A POTAGE OF RYS.

Tak Rys and les hem and wasch hem clene and seth hem tyl they breste and than lat hem kele and seth cast ther'to Almand mylk and colour it wyth safroun and boyle it and messe yt forth.

IX. FOR TO MAKE LAMPREY FRESCH IN GALENTYNE [1].

Schal be latyn blod atte Navel and schald yt and rost yt and ley yt al hole up on a Plater and zyf hym forth wyth Galentyn that be mad of Galyngale gyngener and canel and dresse yt forth.

[1] This is a made or compounded thing. See both here, and in the next Number, and v. Gloss.

X. FOR TO MAKE SALT LAMPREY IN GALENTYNE [1].

Yt schal be stoppit [2] over nyzt in lews water and in braan and flowe and sodyn and pyl onyons and seth hem and ley hem al hol by the Lomprey and zif hem forthe wyth galentyne makyth [3] wyth strong vyneger and wyth paryng of wyt bred and boyle it al togeder' and serve yt forthe.

[1] See note [1] on the last Number. [2] Perhaps, *steppit*, i. e. steeped. See No. 12. [3] Perhaps, *makyd*, i.e. made.

XI. FOR TO MAKE LAMPREYS IN BRUET.

They schulle be schaldyd and ysode and ybrulyd upon a gredern and grynd peper and safroun and do ther'to and boyle it and do the Lomprey ther'yn and serve yt forth.

XII. FOR TO MAKE A STORCHOUN.

He schal be shorn in besys [1] and stepyd [2] over nyzt and sodyn longe as Flesch and he schal be etyn in venegar.

[1] Perhaps, *pesys*, i.e. pieces. [2] Qu. *steppit*, i.e. steeped.

XIII. FOR TO MAKE SOLYS IN BRUET.

They schal be fleyn and sodyn and rostyd upon a gredern and grynd Peper and Safroun and ale boyle it wel and do the sole in a plater and the bruet above serve it forth.

XIV. FOR TO MAKE OYSTRYN IN BRUET.

They schul be schallyd [1] and ysod in clene water grynd peper safroun bred and ale and temper it wyth Broth do the Oystryn ther'ynne and boyle it and salt it and serve it forth.

[1] Have shells taken off.

XV. FOR TO MAKE ELYS IN BRUET.

They schul be flayn and ket in gobett' and sodyn and grynd peper and safroun other myntys and persele and bred and ale and temper it wyth the broth and boyle it and serve it forth.

XVI. FOR TO MAKE A LOPISTER.

He schal be rostyd in his scalys in a ovyn other by the Feer under a panne and etyn wyth Veneger.

XVII. FOR TO MAKE PORREYNE.

Tak Prunys fayrist wasch hem wel and clene and frot hem wel in syve for the Jus be wel ywronge and do it in a pot and do ther'to wyt gres and a party of sugur other hony and mak hem to boyle togeder' and mak yt thykke with flowr of rys other of wastel bred and wan it is sodyn dresse it into dischis and strew ther'on powder and serve it forth.

XVIII. FOR TO MAKE CHIRESEYE.

Tak Chiryes at the Fest of Seynt John the Baptist and do away the stonys grynd hem in a morter and after frot hem wel in a seve so that the Jus be wel comyn owt and do than in a pot and do ther'in feyr gres or Boter and bred of wastrel ymyid [1] and of sugur a god party and a porcioun of wyn and wan it is wel ysodyn and ydressyd in Dyschis stik ther'in clowis of Gilofr' and strew ther'on sugur.

[1] Perhaps, *ymycid*, i.e. minced; or *mycd*, as in No. 19.

XIX. FOR TO MAKE BLANK DE SUR' [1].

Tak the zolkys of Eggs sodyn and temper it wyth mylk of a kow and do ther'to Comyn and Safroun and flowr' of ris or wastel bred mycd and grynd in a morter and temper it up wyth the milk and mak it boyle and do ther'to wit [2] of Egg' corvyn smale and tak fat chese and kerf ther'to wan the licour is boylyd and serve it forth.

[1] Vide Note [1] on No. 29. of Part I. [2] white. So *wyt* is *white* in No. 21. below.

XX. FOR TO MAKE GRAVE ENFORSE.

Tak tryd [1] gyngener and Safroun and grynd hem in a morter and temper hem up wyth Almandys and do hem to the fir' and wan it boylyth wel do ther'to zolkys of Egg' sodyn and fat chese corvyn in gobettis and wan it is dressid in dischis strawe up on Powder of Galyngale and serve it forth.

[1] It appears to me to be *tryd*. Can it be *fryd*?

XXI. FOR TO MAKE HONY DOUSE [1].

Tak god mylk of Almandys and rys and wasch hem wel in a feyr' vessel and in fayr' hoth water and after do hem in a feyr towayl for to drie and wan that they be drye bray hem wel in a morter al to flowr' and afterward tak two partyis and do the half in a pot and that other half in another pot and colowr that on wyth the safroun and lat that other be wyt and lat yt boyle tyl it be thykke and do ther'to a god party of sugur and after dresse yt in twe dischis and loke that thou have Almandys boylid in water and in safroun and in wyn and after frie hem and set hem upon the fyre sethith mete [2] and strew ther'on sugur that yt be wel ycolouryt [3] and serve yt forth.

[1] See Part II. No. I; and Part I. No. 50. [2] Seth it mete, i.e. seeth it properly. [3] Coloured. See No. 28. below.

XXII. FOR TO MAKE A POTAGE FENEBOILES.

Tak wite benes and seth hem in water and bray the benys in a morter al to nozt and lat them sethe in almande mylk and do ther'in wyn and hony and seth [1] reysons in wyn and do ther'to and after dresse yt forth.

[1] i.e. Seeth.

XXIII. FOR TO MAKE TARTYS IN APPLIS.

Tak gode Applys and gode Spycis and Figys and reysons and Perys and wan they are wel ybrayed colourd [1] wyth Safroun wel and do yt in a cofyn and do yt forth to bake wel.

[1] Perhaps, *coloure*.

XXIV. FOR TO MAKE RYS ALKER'.

Tak Figys and Reysons and do awey the Kernelis and a god party of Applys and do awey the paryng of the Applis and the Kernelis and bray hem wel in a morter and temper hem up with Almande mylk and menge hem wyth flowr of Rys that yt be wel chariaunt and strew ther'upon powder of Galyngale and serve yt forth.

XXV. FOR TO MAKE TARTYS OF FYSCH OWT OF LENTE.

Mak the Cowche of fat chese and gyngener and Canel and pur' crym of mylk of a Kow and of Helys ysodyn and grynd hem wel wyth Safroun and mak the chowche of Canel and of Clowys and of Rys and of gode Spycys as other Tartys fallyth to be.

XXVI. FOR TO MAKE MORREY [1].

Requir' de Carnibus ut supra [2].

[1] Vide Part I. No. 37. [2] Part I. No. 37.

XXVII. FOR TO MAKE FLOWNYS [1] IN LENTE.

Tak god Flowr and mak a Past and tak god mylk of Almandys and flowr of rys other amydoun and boyle hem togeder' that they be wel chariaud wan yt is boylid thykke take yt up and ley yt on a feyr' bord so that yt be cold and wan the Cofyns ben makyd tak a party of and do upon the coffyns and kerf hem in Schiveris and do hem in god mylk of Almandys and Figys and Datys and kerf yt in fowr partyis and do yt to bake and serve yt forth.

[1] Perhaps, *Flawnes,* or Custards. Chaucer, vide *Slaunis*. Fr. *Flans.*

XXVIII. FOR TO MAKE RAPEE [1].

Tak the Crustys of wyt bred and reysons and bray hem wel in a morter and after temper hem up wyth wyn and wryng hem thorw a cloth and do ther'to Canel that yt be al colouryt of canel and do ther'to hole clowys macys and quibibz the fysch schal be Lucys other Tenchis fryid or other maner Fysch so that yt be fresch and wel yfryed and do yt in Dischis and that rape up on and serve yt forth.

[1] Vide Part I. No. 49.

XXIX. FOR TO MAKE A PORREY CHAPELEYN.

Tak an hundred onyons other an half and tak oyle de Olyf and boyle togeder' in a Pot and tak Almande mylk and boyle yt and do ther'to. Tak and make a thynne Paast of Dow and make therof as it were ryngis tak and fry hem in oyle de Olyve or in wyte grees and boil al togedere.

XXX. FOR TO MAKE FORMENTY ON A FICHSSDAY [1].

Tak the mylk of the Hasel Notis boyl the wete [2] wyth the aftermelk til it be dryyd and tak and coloured [3] yt wyth Safroun and the ferst mylk cast ther'to and boyle wel and serve yt forth.

[1] Fishday. [2] white. [3] Perhaps, *colour*.

XXXI. FOR TO MAKE BLANK DE SYRY [1].

Tak Almande mylk and Flowre of Rys. Tak thereto sugur and boyle thys togedere and dische yt and tak Almandys and wet hem in water of Sugur and drye hem in a panne and plante hem in the mete and serve yt forth.

[1] Vide ad No. 29. of Part I.

XXXII. FOR TO MAKE A PYNADE OR PYVADE.

Take Hony and Rotys of Radich and grynd yt smal in a morter and do yt thereto that hony a quantite of broun sugur and do thereto. Tak Powder of Peper and Safroun and Almandys and do al togedere boyl hem long and hold [1] yt in a wet bord and let yt kele and messe yt and do yt forth [2].

[1] i.e. *keep,* as in next Number. [2] This Recipe is ill expressed.

XXXIII. FOR TO MAKE A BALOURGLY [1] BROTH.

Tak Pikys and spred hem abord and Helys zif thou hast fle hem and ket hem in gobettys and seth hem in alf wyn [2] and half in water. Tak up the Pykys and Elys and hold hem hote and draw the Broth thorwe a Clothe do Powder of Gyngener Peper and Galyngale and Canel into the Broth and boyle yt and do yt on the Pykys and on the Elys and serve yt forth.

[1] This is so uncertain in the original, that I can only guess at it. [2] Perhaps, *alf in wyn,* or dele *in* before *water*.